# Times and Seasons I

# Times and Seasons I

## Homilies for Church Year A

Gellert Memorial Library
St. Patrick's Seminary & University
320 Middlefield Rd.
Menlo Park, CA 94025
library.stpsu.edu

SERGIO P. NEGRO

Edited by Sharon M. Young
Illustrated by Donna Locati

WORDWORKS
Fresno, California

Text © 2001 by the Most Rev. John T. Steinbock,
    Bishop of the Diocese of Fresno, California

Illustrations © 2001 by Donna Castelazo Locati

*All rights reserved. Printed in the United States of America. No part of this book may be used or reproduced in any manner whatsoever without written permission, except in the case of brief quotations embodied in critical articles and reviews. For information contact the publisher, address below, or call (559) 222-9278.*

Cover: "Children of the Light"

Library of Congress Control Number: 2001 129312

ISBN: 0-9641404-4-6

This book was set electronically in Adobe Caslon type. Paper is Georgia Pacific Proterra, an acid-free, 60 percent recycled stock. Printed by Jostens, Visalia, California.

Published by WORDWORKS
*An imprint of*:
Sixth Street Press
3943 N. Sixth Street
Fresno, California 93726

# Contents

| | |
|---|---|
| FOREWORD | ix |
| AUTHOR'S INTRODUCTION | xii |
| REMEMBERING FATHER SERGIO NEGRO | xvi |
| FROM THE EDITOR | xviii |
| THE JESUS OF HISTORY<br>First Sunday of Advent | 1 |
| MAKING PEACE<br>Second Sunday of Advent | 6 |
| ARE YOU THE ONE WHO IS TO COME?<br>Third Sunday of Advent | 10 |
| ACCEPTING WHAT WE CANNOT UNDERSTAND<br>Fourth Sunday of Advent | 14 |
| LIVING IN THE LIGHT.<br>Christmas Eve | 20 |
| CHRISTMAS WORD<br>Christmas Day | 23 |
| THE FAMILY AS BASE CHURCH<br>Feast of the Holy Family | 28 |
| WHO SHALL BE SAVED?<br>Feast of the Epiphany | 32 |
| THE MEANING OF OUR BAPTISM<br>Baptism of the Lord | 36 |
| GROWING IN ORDINARY TIME<br>Second Sunday in Ordinary Time | 41 |
| WORKING FOR THE KINGDOM<br>Third Sunday in Ordinary Time | 45 |
| CHOOSING POVERTY<br>Fouth Sunday in Ordinary Time | 50 |

| | |
|---|---:|
| FEAST OF FOOLS<br>Fifth Sunday in Ordinary Time | 54 |
| FACING TEMPTATION<br>First Sunday of Lent | 58 |
| COMING DOWN FROM THE MOUNTAINTOP<br>Second Sunday of Lent | 62 |
| WOMEN PRIESTS?<br>Third Sunday of Lent | 66 |
| LIVING WITH THE MYSTERY<br>Fourth Sunday of Lent | 70 |
| THE CRUISE SHIP OF LIFE<br>Fifth Sunday of Lent | 75 |
| GIVING THANKS FOR THE EUCHARIST<br>Holy Thursday | 78 |
| IN THE SHADOW OF THE CROSS<br>Good Friday | 80 |
| OUR PART IN THE STORY<br>Easter Vigil | 85 |
| THE CHRIST OF FAITH<br>Easter Sunday | 88 |
| THE REQUIREMENTS OF COMMUNITY<br>Second Sunday of Easter | 93 |
| WALKING WITH THE RISEN LORD<br>Third Sunday of Easter | 97 |
| THE LORD IS MY SHEPHERD<br>Fourth Sunday of Easter | 102 |
| EMPOWERED BY THE RESURRECTION<br>Fifth Sunday of Easter | 106 |
| IF YOU LOVE ME<br>Sixth Sunday of Easter | 110 |

| | |
|---|---|
| THE COSMIC CHRIST<br>    Seventh Sunday of Easter | 113 |
| USING OUR GIFTS<br>    The Feast of Pentecost | 117 |
| AT A LOSS FOR WORDS<br>    Trinity Sunday | 121 |
| SHARING SLOW FOOD<br>    Body and Blood of Christ | 125 |
| WHAT ARE WE DOING HERE?<br>    Tenth Sunday in Ordinary Time | 129 |
| HOW DARE YOU TREAT ME THAT WAY!<br>    Twelfth Sunday in Ordinary Time | 133 |
| WELCOMING THE STRANGER<br>    Thirteenth Sunday in Ordinary Time | 138 |
| THE IDEAL OF HUMILITY<br>    Fourteenth Sunday in Ordinary Time | 142 |
| TAKING ROOT IN GOD'S WORD<br>    Fifteenth Sunday in Ordinary Time | 144 |
| WEEDS IN OUR GARDENS<br>    Sixteenth Sunday in Ordinary Time | 149 |
| MAKE A WISH<br>    Seventeenth Sunday in Ordinary Time | 154 |
| SHARING OUR GIFTS<br>    Eighteenth Sunday in Ordinary Time | 157 |
| THE SOUND OF SILENCE<br>    Nineteenth Sunday in Ordinary Time | 161 |
| CHRISTIAN INCLUSIVENESS<br>    Twentieth Sunday in Ordinary Time | 164 |
| FOR BETTER AND FOR WORSE<br>    Twenty-first Sunday in Ordinary Time | 168 |

COMING TO TERMS WITH THE CROSS
    Twenty-second Sunday in Ordinary Time         173

SAYS WHO?
    Twenty-third Sunday in Ordinary Time          177

OUR NEED TO FORGIVE
    Twenty-fourth Sunday in Ordinary Time         181

IT'S NOT FAIR!
    Twenty-fifth Sunday in Ordinary Time          186

BIG TALK, NO DO
    Twenty-sixth Sunday in Ordinary Time          190

LABORING IN THE VINEYARD
    Twenty-seventh Sunday in Ordinary Time        193

RSVP: COME TO THE BANQUET
    Twenty-eighth Sunday in Ordinary Time         196

OVERCOMING INDIVIDUALISM
    Twenty-ninth Sunday in Ordinary Time          200

NEIGHBORS BEHIND WALLS
    Thirtieth Sunday in Ordinary Time             204

THE CHRISTIAN HALL OF FAME
    Thirty-first Sunday in Ordinary Time          208

COME TO THE PARTY!
    Thirty-second Sunday in Ordinary Time         212

MULTIPLYING OUR TALENTS
    Thirty-third Sunday in Ordinary Time          216

WILL YOU BE PART OF THE KINGDOM?
    Christ the King                               220

NOTES                                             223

INDEX                                             230

# Foreword

Early in 1994, I was approached about succeeding Father Sergio Negro as pastor of St. Paul Newman Center Catholic Church in Fresno. After the initial shock wore off, I thought, "How can I ever be expected to fill this man's shoes?" After all, Father Negro had not only founded and built the Newman Center thirty years earlier, but also had been its only pastor for the same number of years and had become a virtual icon in the local Catholic community. He was one of the few priests who had earned a doctoral degree, was well known in academic and ecumenical circles, and excelled as a teacher and preacher of the Word. Needless to say, I was much relieved when he assured me that he was taking his shoes with him!

Father Negro had a way with words. For a man who came to this country with little or no English-speaking skill, he came to command the language in a way that inspired congregations from the pulpit and touched the hearts of others even in the most casual settings. In many ways he took his cue from St. Paul, who was known to be a powerful proclaimer of the gospel in both the written and spoken word. Like St. Paul, Father Negro was never known to shrink from preaching the truth—even if it should raise some ecclesial eyebrows from time to time.

So well crafted were his homilies that he could touch on the most sensitive and controversial subjects in a way that opened the minds and hearts of his listeners. Yes, there were those who took issue with his homilies, but they knew that they had better be prepared with ample resources and well-reasoned arguments before taking him to task!

Father Negro was truly able to discern the power of words when preaching the Good News in a pastoral way. We need more priests like him. I believe it was St. Francis of Assisi who once said to the friars of his community, "Go out and preach the gospel. Use words only when necessary." To our benefit, Father Negro frequently found it necessary to use words in proclaiming the gospel. Because they were drawn from his personal prayer, study and example of Christian living, the words of his homilies came from and spoke to the heart.

It is my prayer that this selection of Father Negro's homilies, based on cycle A of the lectionary readings (the Gospel of Matthew), will inspire you to believe what you read, teach what you believe, and practice what you teach.

Fr. Perry J. Kavookjian<br>
Fresno, California

# Author's Introduction
## Adapted from Introduction to *Times and Seasons*
### Selection of Homilies from Years A, B & C, Published in May 1994

I have been a priest for more than forty years, and for most of these forty years I have preached at Sunday liturgies. When I look at the boxes and the binders that hold my notes and my homilies for all these years, I wonder what I would find, if I were to go back and look at all those words. I wonder what these notes and writings would reveal about me and the changes that have taken place in my thinking, in my feelings, in the way I experience the presence and the action of God in my life.

I have lived through the profound changes that the Second Vatican Council initiated in the Church and in the liturgy. I have gone from the doctrinal and moral "sermon" to the "homily," a reflection on and application of the Scripture readings for the particular Sunday. I started with an approach to the sacred texts of our Hebrew and Christian traditions that could only be described as "proof-texting," i.e., looking at the biblical writings to find the texts to prove the thesis that I was proposing. I have come to love, respect, and treasure the sacred texts as a rich source of wisdom and knowledge, challenge and comfort, as unsurpassed expressions of faith in the holy mystery of God.

I believe that the God of Abraham, Isaac, and Jacob, and the God of Jesus of Nazareth, has revealed himself in historical events and historical persons, and that these encounters with the living God—experienced, remembered, told, and retold in faith—have been passed on to us for countless generations through the written word and the living faith of the church community and of every faith-filled and grace-filled person who has read or heard the Word of God.

Preaching has never been easy for me, and neither the preparation nor the presentation of the Sunday homily seems to have become easier over the years. If anything, they have become more difficult. It was simpler to hunt for the verse

that said what I wanted to say, much simpler than to listen to the Scripture texts with mind and heart open to the encounter with the God who is willing to lift the veil of his mystery ever so slightly, so that we can be touched by the depth of his infinity and the immediacy of his love.

When I first started my ministry of preaching I used to prepare my sermons on Saturday afternoons or evenings. Now I begin my preparation on Monday of each week, by reading the biblical texts and a number of commentaries and homily helps, to which I am deeply indebted, much more than the references indicate. I let the texts become part of my reflection and my prayer for a couple of days. I often begin to write on Wednesday afternoons, and take Thursday mornings to complete the homily. I continue to think about it, read it again a couple of times, and make changes before I deliver it. And every time, when the process is completed, I feel that I have not done justice to the richness and the beauty of the texts and to the divine mystery that wants to reveal itself to me and through me.

I don't know how many of you are familiar with the way our cycle of liturgical readings is arranged. We have a three-year cycle based on the synoptic Gospels (Matthew, Mark, and Luke). In cycle A, we read the Gospel of Matthew, in cycle B, the Gospel of Mark, and in cycle C, the Gospel of Luke. During the Lenten and Easter seasons, most of the Gospel readings are from the Gospel of John.✝

I would like to dedicate this collection of homilies to the people of St. Paul Newman Center. They are the ones who were always on my mind and in my heart, as I struggled to choose what to say and how to say it, although I always included myself among the listeners because I need to listen just as much as they do.

The people of the parish community are the ones who nourished me over these many years with their experience of faith, who encouraged me, challenged me, and inspired me with their responses and reactions. I am grateful to all, but especially to those who had the courage to tell me not only when they liked the homily and were touched by it, but also when they found it objectionable or difficult to accept.

The final and total credit must be given to the Holy Spirit who guided me and inspired me and corrected me. It is the Spirit who works the wonders of understanding and illumination and transformation in the listeners and in me. This is never more evident to me than on the many occasions when someone would tell me how touched he or she was by something that I had said in the homily, which I did not remember saying or positively had never said. Only the Spirit can perform such wonders!

I pray that the Spirit of God will continue to work through the written word to bring forth an abundant harvest of faith and hope, of understanding and holy imagination, of peace and joy, of tenderness and love in all of us.

*Fergo Negro*

Easter 1994

---

✝This paragraph was part of Father Negro's homily for July 28, 1991, the Seventeenth Sunday in Ordinary Time (Year B).

# Prayer

*Sergio P. Negro*

Who do I pray to you, O Lord my God?
    Because my life is fragile
    and my living a risk
Why do I call your name, O Lord my God?
    Because you know me,
    even better than I know myself,
    and you call me by my name,
    tenderly and gently, softly and lovingly.
    People have heard you in the rolling thunder and
    in the flash of lightning, in the rush of wind
    and in the ocean roar
    but also
    in the gentle rain and the rustle of leaves
    in the quiet space and the peaceful heart.
    Hear my calling you, O Lord, and answer me.
Why do I speak to you, O Lord my God?
    Because I believe you listen and you understand
    Because I know my weakness and my need:
    I need your grace, which is your love
    and I need your presence, which is my strength
Because I need you
    to be all that I can be
    to do all that must be done
    to give all that I can share
        for the sake of human life
        for the sake of our world
        for the sake of all your creation.
This is my prayer, Lord.
So let it be, by your gracious power.
Amen.

## Remembering Father Sergio Negro

In my many fond memories of the forty-five years in which I was privileged to know Father Sergio P. Negro, one theme comes to mind: hunger. I believe hunger—physical, emotional, intellectual, and spiritual—played a key role in shaping Father Negro as a human being and in directing his unique ministry.

Father Negro understood physical hunger deeply. He was born to a humble family of modest means in the Piemonte region of northern Italy. He grew up during the Depression in a country whose economy was suffering the effects of two world wars. Throughout his childhood and adolescence, there was only enough food for basic sustenance. Times became so difficult during World War II that he was sent home from the seminary because the priests no longer had food for their students. He never recovered from these experiences. Even though he lived his entire adult life in the United States surrounded by abundance, the fear of scarcity never left him: He always finished everything on his plate.

Balancing these memories of hunger was his excellent appetite for fine foods, both as a diner and as an accomplished cook. He loved to eat well, and he often encouraged those dining with him to slow down and savor the fruits of good fortune.

World War II took a heavy toll on Father Negro's family. In the Piemonte, it was difficult to know who was aligned with the fascist regime of Benito Mussolini and who was associated with the Christian Democrats. This caused tremendous tension within families and among neighbors. Intimate conversations were limited to confidants within the household, and emotion and affection were never overt.

In spite of this early experience of emotional hunger, Father Negro sought deep connections with his fellow human beings throughout his ministry. In his homilies, as you will read in this volume, he gave tremendously of himself, always striving to reveal his innermost thoughts and feelings. But even at the end of his life he had difficulty showing his emotions, although he cared deeply for many people and considered them his friends.

Father Negro had an insatiable intellectual hunger. He was a dedicated student and voracious reader. One of his great frustrations was that he couldn't know everything. He was in no way a dilettante, flitting from subject to subject and gaining only a superficial understanding. On the contrary, he would immerse himself fully in a subject with the intention of understanding every detail and comprehending every concept. I remember one evening when he was particularly frustrated because he could not understand Einstein's theory of relativity. With his responsibilities as full-time pastor of the Newman Center and part-time professor at California State University, Fresno, he just did not have the time to delve as deeply into subjects as he would have liked.

Nothing was as important to Father Negro as his relationship with his God. He pursued every aspect of spirituality in his life: in his vocation, in academics, in his personal relationships, and in his private times of prayer, meditation, and reflection. It was not sufficient for him to be a man of the cloth or to merely understand great spiritual concepts. Father Negro practiced the precepts of Jesus every day of his life, without regard to the cost. There were many times when he was physically, intellectually, and emotionally exhausted, but he would never turn away a person in need.

Father Negro looked for and found the light in each individual he encountered. Through reaching our hearts, he knew he could connect with our souls. And once connected with our souls, he knew he was connected with God.

Shirley Canales<br>St. Helena, California

## From the Editor

The publication of this volume completes our collection of the homilies of Father Sergio Negro, delivered over a period of nearly thirty years in the Diocese of Fresno, California. Most of these homilies were prepared for the congregation of St. Paul Newman Center, which Father Negro founded in 1964 and served until 1994, when he accepted the position of Vicar General for the diocese. He died on April 18, 1999, at the age of seventy. His death stunned and saddened the parishioners, friends, colleagues, and community members whom he had loved and served for so many years. Reflecting on the loss of his pastor and friend two days after Father Negro's death, Tom Castelazo wrote:

"Father Negro came to Fresno when I was in high school, or perhaps junior high. We would go to St. Therese and he would speak with a thick Italian accent, and we would come away with no idea of what he had said. Over more than forty years he worked on that, cultivated and became clear in his speech, and along the way created a voice, a speech pattern, like no other. It is in my head and will not go away, but I will hear it no more, and I am sad.

"When I was fed up, he was the difference between my remaining in the church and leaving. He had an artistic sense. He thought deeply. He took risks. He challenged the establishment. Now and then he would speak from the pulpit of his personal feelings, his deep aspirations and disappointments. He took a risk doing this, and these were his most endearing homilies.

"Father Negro struggled with contradictions, with the unknown, with uncertainty. He despised the hypocrisy, the control games, the power-seeking, in the church establishment, but he hung in and did not leave. He told me he would like to go to South America and work among the poor, but he hung in there and did not leave. He longed to have a wife and family, but he hung in there and did not leave. And so he died, as all people do, unfulfilled. He did not do all he would have liked to do. Yet he did more than most.

"The great and powerful will gather at his grave, though he had little use for them, take possession of him, and pronounce his life a grand success. And we will hear much about him, and we may go back and read his homilies. But never will we hear his voice again."

Through this volume of homilies for cycle A, and the companion volumes for cycles B and C, those who heard Father Negro's voice, as well as those who did not, have the opportunity to learn from and be inspired by a man who lives on in the people he continues to touch through his words.

The homilies in this collection were selected from homilies Father Negro preached during cycle A between 1972 and 1998. Ten of them appeared in the original volume, *Times and Seasons,* published in 1994 and now out of print. The homilies are arranged according to the Sundays and feast days of the year 2001–2002. The early date of Easter in 2002 corresponds to only one other year in this cycle for which homilies were available, 1975, with the result that we have no homily for the Eleventh Sunday in Ordinary Time. In 1975, Father Negro had a guest speaker on that Sunday!

In his homily for the Feast of the Epiphany in 1990, found on page 32, Father Negro shared his inclusive vision:

> God's love is for all, without exceptions. The people whom God favors are chosen not for their own sake, for a privileged position, but for the sake of others—to serve them, to be the light that shines and leads others into the presence, into the mystery of God.... Perhaps we can find ways to promote the common good while respecting the individual good of every person, ways that will unite us rather than isolate us, ways that will build the human family along with individual nations. I believe that these would be new ways of learning and proclaiming the meaning of Jesus Christ and of the salvation that he brought to the world.

As nations, churches, and individuals continue to insist that God's favor rests only on them and those who believe as they do, Father Negro's words and life are a welcome gift of openness and compassion. May these homilies nourish and strengthen us to live out the gospel day by day.

Sharon M. Young, Editor

# The Jesus of History

Time: November 27, 1977
Season: First Sunday of Advent
Scripture Readings: Isaiah 2:1–5; Romans 13:11–14a;
  Matthew 24:37–44

During the new liturgical year which begins today, the cycle of the Gospel readings will draw primarily from the Gospel of Matthew. I wish those responsible for making the Gospel selections would have given us for this Sunday the beginning of Matthew's Gospel, instead of going to one of the last chapters in order to continue the apocalyptic theme of the preceding two Sundays. Today's Gospel reading reminds us that the coming of the Lord for which we are still waiting is the final coming of the Son of Man in glory.

The Gospel of Matthew begins with a genealogy, in the verses we will read on Christmas Eve. These are the verses we need to make an important point for the beginning of our Advent journey. Both Matthew and Luke used genealogies to make the point that Jesus has a concrete history, earthly roots, historical ancestors. The genealogy in Matthew 1:1–25 is not an accurate historical record. Rather, it reflects the working out of God's plan of creation in and through a history of salvation. The particular names and details are not the important part.

Matthew begins his genealogy with the words: "The book of the genealogy of Jesus Christ, the son of David, the son of Abraham." This is the family of Jesus. Jesus is a Jew, a son of Abraham, a descendant of David, the great king, the symbol of the chosen ruler, the one who had received the promise that one of his descendants would be God's representative, God's appointed king over his people.

There is a richness and depth of thought in the way the Gospel writers convey to us the human, earthly dimension of Jesus' being and life that is difficult for us to grasp. As "the son of Abraham," Jesus is not everyman, some kind of ideal or universal man, a person born at random into the family of man.

Jesus has a specific identity within a historical group, the Israelites. Abraham represents the origin of the people of Israel. He was the first one to receive the promise, the first to live in faith in Yahweh, trusting a faithful God. Jesus belongs to Abraham's people. He embodies the promise; he lives to a new depth of meaning the attitude of faithful trust in the saving God. Notice how many times Abraham's name recurs in the Gospels, often in situations that touch on the question of the identity of Jesus, of who Jesus is.

In early Christian thought there is a deep-rooted parallelism between Jesus and Moses. In the infancy narratives in Matthew, Jesus is taken to Egypt and returns from there to the land of Israel. The parallelism is used to point to Jesus as the new lawgiver. The Law that came to the Israelites through Moses was an inescapable part of Jesus' identity and life, from the stories of his infancy to his sentence of death.

The covenant of Sinai was the other powerful presence that came to Jesus from Mosaic times. Jesus comes from a people who see themselves existing in a mutual relationship with God. The God whom Jesus calls Father is the Yahweh of the covenant, and throughout his ministry Jesus is aware that the people whom he is addressing are God's special people. After his death and resurrection, when his disciples are trying to express Jesus' significance, they describe him as the "new covenant."

One of the major New Testament themes is that Jesus is a descendant of David. Matthew makes the first major break in his genealogy with "David the king." He concludes the genealogy with Joseph, making clear that Joseph is not the physical father of Jesus. Matthew builds his story to affirm, without any possibility of doubt, that Joseph is the legal father of Jesus. By taking Mary as his wife he claims her child as his own, and he is instructed to name the child. Legal paternity has a much deeper and stronger meaning in Jewish tradition than it would have for us now. There was no significant difference between biological and legal paternity. At times, legal paternity even overshadowed biological paternity.

By calling Jesus "son of David," Matthew establishes Jesus' legitimate claim to lead God's people. He has a right to the scepter, to the power and authority, of the great king, according to the promise of the prophet Nathan to David. Jesus' roots reach back through the centuries to the glories and the shame of David and Solomon and the long line of kings that leads to the occupation of the land, the destruction of Jerusalem and its temple, and the exile into Babylon.

The second major break in Matthew's genealogy is the Babylonian exile, a time of great loss and tragedy, of hopelessness and near despair. But this was also the time of Jeremiah and Second Isaiah, a time of deepening faith and a new understanding of the uniqueness of Yahweh and his relationship to his people. The prophetic word becomes a word of comfort and consolation. It speaks of new hopes; it offers new and magnificent vistas of the future salvation that God prepares for his people. It is a time of interiority, the emergence of personal and individual faith, and, above all, a new understanding of the meaning and redemptive power of suffering.

The sorrows and pains and wounds of the faithful people would give rise to the mysterious and tender figure of the Suffering Servant of Yahweh. This figure would supply the first title that the Christian community assigned to Jesus in their faith born of the Resurrection, probably because Jesus had identified himself so closely with the image and ideal of the Suffering Servant.

I have given you just a glimpse of the richness and depth of the human and historical roots of Jesus. I would urge you to take the time to read from the Old Testament during the coming days of Advent, from the patriarchal stories in the book of Genesis, from the story of Moses in Exodus (especially his encounter with God at the mountain of the covenant), and from the second book of Samuel and the stories of David (probably some of the best literature that human creativity has produced and human imagination recorded), from Jeremiah and Second Isaiah (chapters 40 to 55 of the book of Isaiah).

I wish I could share with you what I know and what I feel about these ancient peoples and events. They make Jesus come alive for me in a new light. The reality, the concreteness of his humanity assume new power and meaning in the context of Matthew's efforts to place Jesus in a very specific historical context. I would like to suggest that we take the time during Advent to look at our own roots, to see how our heritage has touched and shaped us from the moment of our birth. It is true that each human person is a new creation, but the decision of freedom that makes us what we are operates in the context of what is already there, of what others have made us, of what the past has given us. This was true of Jesus, and it is true of us.

## Making Peace

TIME: DECEMBER 4, 1983
SEASON: SECOND SUNDAY OF ADVENT
SCRIPTURE READINGS: ISAIAH 11:1–10; ROMANS 15:4–9; MATTHEW 3:1–12

Paul's wish for the Christian community at Rome, that they may "think in harmony with one another, in keeping with Christ Jesus," would not have been easy to achieve. He was writing to them in a situation of tension and conflict over food and drink, over the observance of the Sabbath. In the verses preceding today's reading he urges the Christians at Rome to "no longer pass judgment on one another" (14:13), and to "pursue what makes for peace and for mutual upbuilding" (14:19). He instructs them: "We who are strong ought to put up with the failings of the weak, and not to please ourselves. Each of us must please our neighbor for the good purpose of building up the neighbor" (15:1–2).

Peace, harmony, and mutual acceptance do not come easily, even in the Christian community. Peace, justice, faithfulness, freedom from fear and destruction—these are the deepest longings of the human heart, of human communities. The first reading from Isaiah is an expression of these longings. At a time when the nation was threatened with destruction and impending desolation, Isaiah has a vision of a great leader who would establish universal harmony. No longer would people and nations "fight like cats and dogs," but, in the familiar words, "the calf and the young lion shall browse together, and a little child shall lead them." We relish Isaiah's magnificent description of the whole of creation living together as one family in peace.

As Christians, we interpret the prophetic word of Isaiah as fulfilled in Jesus Christ. But what happened to the vision of peace and harmony for all of creation? It will not be realized without us. We can either block it and delay it, or we can work for it and bring it closer to fulfillment.

The Gospel reflects the insistent call to reform, change of heart, repentance. John calls the people to "Repent, for the kingdom of heaven is at hand!" The long hoped for, expected kingdom of God is near; it awaits the change in us that will allow it to be established and to flourish. We must prepare the way of the Lord.

Mother Teresa once pointed out: "The greatest poverty is right in our own homes.... Know the poor of your own family." She understood that at times it is easier to see Christ in the poor dying in the streets than in the people with whom we live every day. She said: "It is easier to offer rice to the poor than to fill the loneliness of someone lacking love in our own family." Her suggestion is simple: "Make your home another Nazareth where peace, love, and joy reign.... Let us begin in the place where we are, with the people to whom we are the closest, and spread out."

Today I would like to invite you to look at the ideal and goal of peace in your own family, in the small communities of which you are a part. Is there a need for reconciliation, for actively working for and building peace and harmony?

Dr. David Thomas of St. Regis College in Denver deals with this challenge in an article on "The Family and Reconciliation." He suggests that when problems arise—a broken lamp, someone leaving the water running, a missing toy—we can deal with them in several different ways. The first way is by denying responsibility for the problem. Nobody really wants to admit mistakes or hurtful behavior. A second response is to blame another person for causing the problem, or for causing us to behave improperly. Thomas suggests that reconciliation requires some form of confession and acceptance of responsibility, and that the problem must be solved. He indicates that many processes of reconciliation stop here, but that two further steps are necessary.

In addition to a physical solution—fixing the lamp, turning off the water, finding the toy—there needs to be an interpersonal solution, a mending of relationships with a loving word, an offer to help, an act of kindness toward another person. Finally, according to Thomas, we must achieve closure.

The incident is over, finished. It is time to start again with a clean slate. He suggests some symbolic event that signifies that things are back to normal—a hug, a note, sharing a meal.

Can you think of a person with whom you need to be reconciled? Are there old wounds that have not been healed, angry words that have not been taken back, things that have not been returned, problems that have not been resolved? Today's Scripture readings invite us to take the initiative to make peace happen and continue. Don't wait for the other person. Each of us is called to be a peacemaker. Peace is born from what we do. It is not something we wait for, expecting somebody else to initiate it. The season of Advent calls for an attitude, an effort, a dedication to peace.

If we want a new world, a world like the one described by Isaiah, we can't just continue to blame others for the mess we are in. We can't keep waiting for others to change and fix things up. Let there be peace in our families, and let it begin with me. Let there be peace on Earth, and let it begin with me.

## Are You the One Who Is to Come?

TIME: DECEMBER 11, 1977
SEASON: THIRD SUNDAY OF ADVENT
SCRIPTURE READINGS: ISAIAH 35:1–6A, 10; JAMES 5:7–10;
    MATTHEW 11:2–11

If you had your choice, in what historical age would you like to live? Did you ever ask yourself this question? Many years ago, in the early fifties, I remember saying that I would have liked to be born in the Middle Ages. Why? Because until the 1960s and the Second Vatican Council, many Catholics would look back on the Middle Ages as the golden age of the Church, as the period of greatest strength and glory for the Christian establishment.

It was the age of faith, where everyone at least appeared to hold the same beliefs. It was the age of Christendom, a time as close to the unity of religious, political, cultural, and popular life under the rule of Christ as could ever be achieved. Perhaps the rule was more that of the Pope and bishops, of ecclesiastical authority, than of Christ, but there were some great and holy popes and bishops. Religious, spiritual authority was supreme. It crowned kings and emperors; it controlled life here on earth; it held the keys to unlock the doors for the next life in heaven; it could call upon the secular powers to keep the faith pure and to punish sinners and heretics; it could even gather armies for holy wars against unbelievers in order to regain possession of the land made holy by the life and death of the humble Galilean who now was acclaimed as Christ the king. It was the age of saints. Motivated by Christian charity, innumerable men and women lived lives of service and sacrifice for the sake of others.

As Roman Catholics, we looked back on the Middle Ages in the same way as the Jews at the time of Jesus looked back on the memories of the great kingdoms of David and Solomon as the ideal moment of history. Like the Jews at the time of Jesus, who hoped for a restoration of the ancient kingdom and all its glories, many of us were hoping for a return of the age of faith and Christendom, the age of the saints and of the rule of the spiritual. We looked back on the Middle Ages as a time of fulfillment of all that we expected for the new people of God, and we hoped for its return.

I do not know if any of you ever felt in any way what I have just described. But I do know that, consciously or unconsciously, we had distorted the meaning of the kingdom of God in Jesus Christ and we, too, the Church, had become a messianic people in an earthly sense, as if the kingdom had been realized and become identical with the Church; as if the Church, rather than Jesus, had become the instrument of salvation, the keeper of the promises; as if the Church, rather than the promises of God, had become the hope of a new world.

Now perhaps we are confused (I know, there is evidence, that many people are), as John the Baptist was. We ask of the Church, as he did of Christ: "Are you the one who is to come or should we look for another?" People outside of the Church have asked the same question of the Church, not just of the institution but also of its members: Are you truly a disciple of Jesus? Do you really believe in the teachings of him whom you call Lord? Then why do you do the things that you do? How can you behave as you do?

Is that a legitimate question? Yes. In the First Letter of Peter we read: "But you are a chosen race, a royal priesthood, a holy nation, God's own people, in order that you may proclaim the mighty acts of him who called you out of darkness into his marvelous light. Once you were not a people, but now you are God's people; once you had not received mercy, but now you have received mercy" (1 Pet. 2:9–10).

The believing community, the faithful disciples, are the continuing historical presence of the mystery of God's saving grace in Jesus Christ, the concrete and visible signs of the redeeming love of Jesus, the sacrament of God's salvation. We are the messianic people, the people of the new promises and new hopes. But in our historical development we seem to have fulfilled the old promises, the old hopes. We seem to have fulfilled the expectations of the people in the time of Christ, without the radical change in understanding that Jesus brought.

We developed a new code of laws that was even more detailed and even more rigid than the old law, the Mosaic Law. We developed a new system of ritual, a new priestly class just as jealous of its prerogatives as the descendants of Aaron who served the Jerusalem temple. And we acted as if the observance of the law and the magic of ritual were the saving power, rather than the free gift and the overflowing love and the gentle power of God in Jesus Christ. We developed an establishment, an earthly institution, and then proceeded to equate it with the kingdom of God.

What I am sharing with you today are ideas that would not even have crossed my mind fifteen years ago. We are in a new season, a new Advent, a time of new hopes and expectations. What are we waiting for? For the mystery of Christ to renew itself in us for our time, for us and for our world. What is this mystery?

Jesus did not align himself with the powers of the establishment or become a defender of the status quo. Jesus did not take up the cause of the military rebels and did not let himself be co-opted into the cause of revolution. Jesus did not retreat from the wicked world to lead a group of ascetic monks into a life of penance and sacrifice. Jesus did not compromise and adapt his message so that it could be acceptable and popular.

Jesus spoke the truth as he saw it. If he did start a revolution, it was the revolution of nonviolence, of loving service and humble acceptance even of death for the sake of others. He confronted the evils of the world to heal them and to forgive them. Jesus was absolutely faithful to his mission, to the message that he felt he had received from the Father and had been charged to proclaim: the Good News of God's salvation. As we heard in Isaiah today: "Here is your God, he comes with vindication; with divine recompense he comes to save you."

We, as a Church, as a believing community, will never be a messianic people, a people who can make the promises believable and the hope relevant to our contemporaries, until we follow the example of Jesus, until we too can say, as Jesus said in today's reading from Matthew: "Go and tell John what you hear and see." We will never be such a people until we become ourselves sight for those who cannot see; until we carry the cripples on our shoulders or transport them in our cars, if that is the only way they can move; until we find ways of communicating and helping others communicate; until we find ways to give value to life where there is nothing but death, to make decent, human life possible where living is more like dying; until we become ourselves good news, hope, freedom for the poor and oppressed.

To do this, the Church must be willing to become, to be, to remain provisional and pilgrim, to be a servant, to be the presence of healing and saving in the world, totally committed to its mission in radical conversion to the mystery of love that is in Jesus.

## Accepting What We Cannot Understand

Time: December 20, 1998
Season: Fourth Sunday of Advent
Scripture Readings: Isaiah 7:10–14; Romans 1:1–7; Matthew 1:18–24

Christmas is getting so close that it would be very tempting to look ahead and to anticipate its joy. But it is not Christmas yet! We have a few more days to prepare our hearts for the coming of Jesus. We still have a little work to do to get ready to welcome Jesus into our world once again. We must use these days well.

It is easy to romanticize the story of Christmas, to think of stars and singing angels and little children and warm fires and doors open to welcome family members. But the Gospel reading today invites us to enter into a situation that is quite difficult and painful. Mary and Joseph are engaged to be married, but before they begin to live together, Joseph discovers that Mary is pregnant. There are just simple, ordinary people. It is easy to understand how "Joseph is bewildered, stunned that the young woman with whom his and her parents have arranged a good match for him is pregnant. He may not have known her yet even to speak to—that is the way it was in that culture of arranged marriages—but he knew he was not the father."[1]

According to Mosaic Law, Joseph had the right to divorce Mary publicly. But, as the Gospel tells us, Joseph was a good, just, compassionate, and caring man. He did not want to bring public shame on Mary. After all, she was a very young woman, probably a teenager, and Joseph had no idea of what might have happened to her. Joseph decided to quietly get out of the way, to give Mary her freedom. He must have thought that by doing that, the father of the child could do the right thing and claim Mary as his wife.

But one night an angel of the Lord comes to Joseph in a dream and tells him: "Do not be afraid. This child is the special work of God. Take Mary into your house as your wife and

give a name to this child when he is born." This is how a man in those days claimed his paternity and his rights as a father, by naming the child. I wonder which was the greater shock for Joseph, the bigger challenge to his faith and his righteousness: to discover that Mary was pregnant or to be told that the Holy Spirit of God was responsible for Mary's condition, and that he should act as if this were his own child.

Try to imagine what Joseph's feelings might have been. Try to enter into his heart as he reflects and prays about this extraordinary message that he has received. At the beginning, there must have been a good deal of pain and confusion in Joseph. How could he not ask himself: Whose child is this that I am being asked to acknowledge publicly as my own? What is God asking of me? What will I tell the child about who is his real father? How am I going to raise someone who is going to save the people from their sins, someone who is God-with-us?

In the stories about the birth of Jesus, Joseph is the one who is most like us. He has to face circumstances beyond his control. He is asked to accept a situation and to live his life in a manner that he had not chosen for himself. He is tempted to say: Forget it! I don't want any part of this! He would be tempted to run away, but God does not let him. God tells Joseph: Don't be afraid. I am here with you. It may not be the life you had planned, but this is the way God wants to be born here, if you allow it.[2]

Can you think of a situation in your own life, in the life of a family member, of a good friend, of someone close to you, in which an unexpected pregnancy turned all plans upside down, caused anger, fear, rejection, confusion, uncertainty, and forced people to make decisions they did not want to make?

I wonder how many of you here have chosen to accept as your own a child of whom you are not the biological parent. The meaning of being a parent has changed radically in our society. Maybe it is easier for us to understand what Joseph might have been feeling when he accepted to name Mary's child and so make the child his own son. Today we talk of "blended" families," "voluntary families," "adopted families."

Isn't that what Joseph did? By his acceptance of God's message to him, he became an adoptive father; he created a voluntary family. It was an act of great faith on his part—faith in God, but also faith in Mary, and faith in the family being created.

Christmas will be a day of great joy for many people, but Christmas will also bring intense pain, tears, and sorrow to some people. There are children who enrich our celebration of Christmas beyond compare, children who are wanted, who enrich healthy, happy homes and families, who bring feelings of great joy and profound gratitude. But there are also children who are seen as burdens, who bring anxiety and sorrow, perhaps because of extreme poverty or the inability of single parents to provide for all the needs of their children. There can be great pain for parents who are unable to provide the necessities, let alone buy gifts for their children.

Christmas will see many gatherings where loving marriage partners, children, extended families, relatives, and friends join to celebrate the wonders of hearts and lives united in love and trust and mutual fidelity. But there are also broken marriages, and children torn by conflicting loyalties to separated parents. There are spouses who are alone this year because their partner of many years has been taken by death. I am sure many of us have a spouse, a parent, a son or daughter, a sister or brother, a friend, who will not be with us this year as they have been in years past. Sometimes it seems that God asks some very difficult, painful things of us, things we do not understand, things we can only accept because we want to be faithful to God, who has promised to be with us—just as Joseph is asked to accept Mary's child as his own, without fully understanding what that means and what will be expected of him.

As we continue to prepare for Christmas I think we are asked, as Joseph was, to deepen our faith, to accept our life with all its uncertainties, its difficulties, its seeming absurdities, as a call from God to trust him and to serve him. God is asking to be born again in us and in our world, in and through Jesus' presence within us. And God is born in us when we

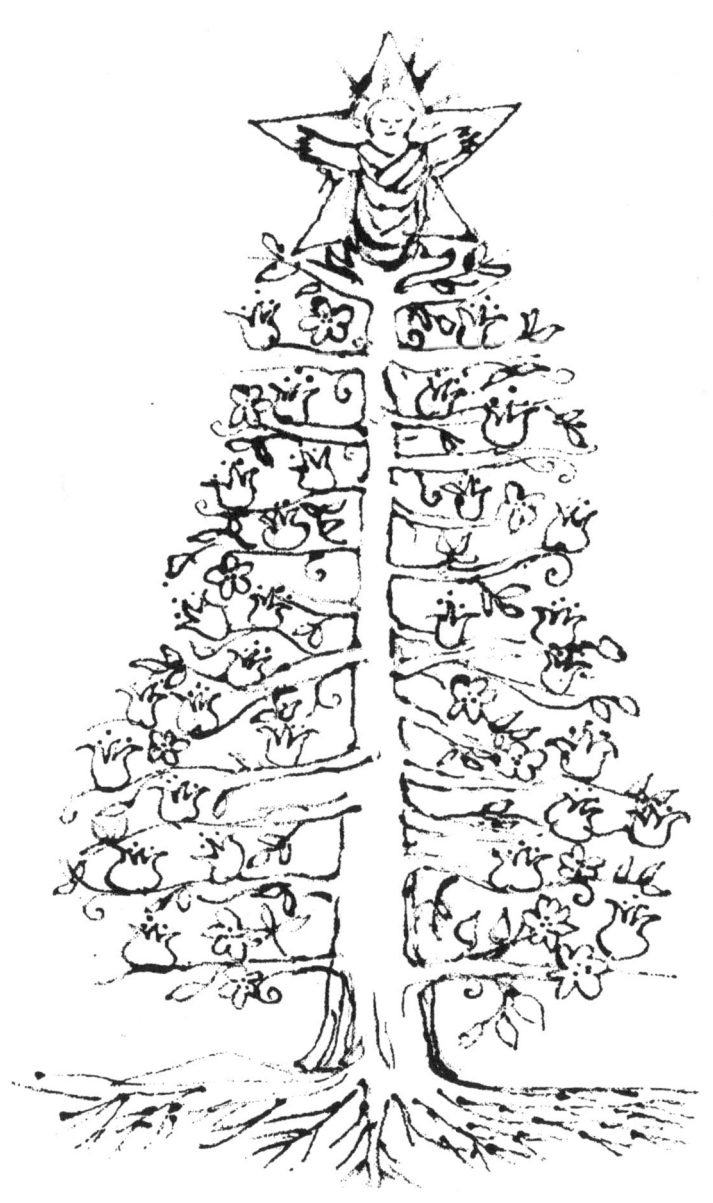

become more present to each other, more aware of each other's pains and sorrows, more helpful to each other in difficult times. God is born in us when we are more accepting and understanding toward each other, when we stretch out our hand in solidarity and offer a friendly smile and welcome each other as signs of God's presence among us.

Today we celebrate Joseph as the one who accepted, protected, and nurtured God's presence in Jesus. Joseph became the bearer of Christ to the world, just as Mary was. Joseph helps us to rejoice and give thanks that Christ asks for a chance to be born again in us, that he invites us to bear his imprint in our hearts and to carry his love with us wherever we go. All we need to do is accept Jesus as our own, just as Joseph accepted him as his own, to name Jesus as our brother, as our Lord and our Savior.

## Living in the Light

TIME: DECEMBER 24, 1998
  (final homily preached at St. Paul Newman Center)
SEASON: CHRISTMAS EVE
SCRIPTURE READINGS: ISAIAH 9:1–6; TITUS 2:11–14;
  LUKE 2:1–14

In these days, when the world seems to be coming apart at the seams, we need a place where we can be at peace with ourselves and with one another, in shared values and mutual support. We need people who can reflect for us the light of Christ that broke through the world's darkness, people who reflect for us the love and compassion of our God who alone can overcome our human sinfulness. On this Christmas Eve we have gathered here to celebrate the light of Christ, to create, with Jesus, such a place of hope, to create such a community of people of light and compassion, by the power of God.

There are many reasons why we might feel that our world is coming apart at the seams. Some of these reasons might be very personal, coming from serious problems we have to face, from struggles that leave us feeling defeated and hopeless. Some reasons come from what is happening in our world, as we learn it from stories and events, and not just from what is shouted in the headlines and lead stories. Often it is the little "News in Brief" items that jolt me with the realization of how terribly cruel we human beings can be to one another.

I receive many appeals for help from missionary groups and dioceses throughout the world. Last week I received a letter from a diocese in Southern Sudan, describing conditions so desperate, treatment so cruel, oppression so inhuman, that it can only be described as a new age of slavery.

The season of Advent and the celebration of Christmas invite us once again to look at the world and ourselves from a different perspective, in a different light. In Christ we hold the promise that God has come into our world to dispel our darkness and to overcome our evil. Today we rejoice in the revelation that God has sent his only begotten Son into our world so that the world might be saved. Because of our faith, we trust that in Christ this is a graced world, a redeemed world, that God's love is stronger than all our capacity for evil. The whole mystery of Christ, from birth to resurrection, is testimony that God's power is stronger than all evil, is witness to God's victory over sin and death, over darkness and evil.

I heard a story about a cave who lived, as caves are wont to do, in the side of a mountain. This particular cave was very unhappy being a cave and complained day and night about her lot. One day, as the sun was passing through the sky, he overheard the cave's complaints.

"What's wrong, Sister Cave?" the sun called out.

"Oh, I am so miserable being a cave," she replied. "It is so dark, so damp and so depressing."

"Your problem," said the sun, "is that you haven't seen the light. What you need to do is to come out of your mountain and experience my marvelous light. Then you'll feel so much better."

"I don't know, Brother Sun," the cave replied. "You just don't understand what it's like having to live in darkness. You have never experienced what I'm going through. How can you offer me advice?"

"Well, maybe you are right. I'll tell you what," said the sun. "We'll make a deal: You come out into my light so that you can see how wonderful it is, then I'll go inside of you so that I can experience the darkness."

The cave thought about the proposition for a while and then agreed to the trade. "O.K.," said the cave. "You go first."

"No, you go first," said the sun.

"No, you first."

"No, you first."

At last the cave agreed to go first. Very slowly she started to come out of the mountain, but the sunlight blinded her and she rushed back into the mountain. Gently, the sun coaxed her back out. Finally she was all out of the mountain and completely in the sunlight. At first, her eyes were blinded and she had to rub them with her hands. Then the cave began to dance with joy.

"You see, I told you that you would feel much better once you came into my light," the sun said. But after a while the cave stopped dancing and began to look very depressed.

"Now what's wrong?" asked the sun.

"Well, you see, life is not all sunlight. In every life there has to be some darkness. And now it is your turn to see what darkness is like."

So the sun asked the cave to go back into her mountain, make herself as dark as she could, and let him know when she was ready. The cave went back in and got herself darker than she had ever been in her entire life. Then she called out to the sun: "O.K., Brother Sun, I'm ready for you. Come and see what darkness is like."

The sun came down from the heavens and rushed inside the cave. Then he called out to her, "O.K., Sister Cave, where is your darkness? Show me your darkness!"

But the cave couldn't. The cave couldn't because the sun was shining so brightly that there was no darkness anywhere.[3]

Life is not all sunlight, and in every life there is darkness. But Christmas reminds us that Jesus has called us to be the light of the world. Christmas is an invitation to look for the light, wherever we may find it, to look for the goodness that is in ourselves and in others, because, in truth, there is light and there is goodness everywhere in the world. We need to search for it, bring it out, let it be seen and admired, so that it can be inspiration and hope, so that it can dispel the darkness.

# Christmas Word

TIME: DECEMBER 25, 1988
SEASON: CHRISTMAS DAY

In the beginning was the Word

   Let there be light and let there be darkness
   Let there be waters and let there be earth
   Let there be things that grow
      seed bearing plants and fruit giving trees
   Let there be sun and let there be moon
   Let there be days and let there be nights
   Let there be birds that fly and fish that swim
   Let there be living creatures upon the earth
      cattle and creeping things and beasts of all kinds
   Let there be man and let there be woman
      and let them our image and likeness be

   Such power in the Word
      for the Word was with God and the Word was God
      all things were made through him
And the word was given to man and to woman too

      I was afraid because I was naked
      the woman gave me the fruit of the tree
      the serpent deceived me and I ate the fruit
      I don't know where my brother is. Am I his keeper?

      and words grew angry and violence multiplied
      and fear spread and wickedness was everywhere
      and evil reigned and the Lord was grieved
      and flood waters came but not forever
      and pride increased and reached up to heaven
      and the words grew many and the tongues confused
      and there were many languages and no understanding

In the Word was life and life brings light
and light shines in darkness and is not overcome

God's Word does not forsake his world
God's Word is not spent in one creation
God's love can speak new words

    words of challenge and confrontation
    words of promise and consolation
    words of pleading and instruction
    words in the starry night
    words from a burning bush
    words like thunder from a mountain storm
    words like silence in a craggy cave
    words like praying king and crying prophet
    words shouted in the wind and written on the stone

And the Word was made flesh and dwelt among us
    and the Word of God now speaks in human words

    change your heart and believe
    God's reign is in your midst
    the Spirit of the Lord is upon me
    your sins are forgiven
    your faith has saved you
    blessed are you poor and you that hunger
        you that weep and are reviled
    love your enemies and do good
        to those who hate you and even curse you
    take up your cross and follow me
    do this and remember me
    love one another as I have loved you
    Father forgive them for they know not
    my God why have you forsaken me
    I am the resurrection and the life
    I am the light of the world
    do not be afraid for peace is my gift
    as the Father has sent me so I send you
    You shall be my witnesses to the ends of the earth

And we have beheld his glory
    glory as of the only Son from the Father

## Christmas Word

in the darkness of night and in the light of stars
in the noonday sun and in the shapeless clouds
in the crashing ocean surf and in the whispering leaves
in the first cry of a newborn baby
in the last sigh of a dying wo/man
in the words of scripture and in the bread of communion
in the waters of new life and the oil of healing

when we gave bread to the hungry
    and drink to the thirsty
    and shelter to the homeless
    and comfort to the sorrowing
    and hope to the prisoner
    and welcome to the stranger
for his glory is in the least ones
    of his brothers and sisters
when we love one another as he has loved us

And from his fullness we have all received
    grace upon grace, gift upon gift
        fullness of truth and of life
            and his Word can be heard in our words

merry christmas and a happy new year
a joy that is holy and a peace that is true
a life that is graced and a death that is crown
friends that are faithful knocking at your door

family that is loving gathered at your table
happiness that makes you humble before the Lord
sorrows that lead you to find his presence again

thank you for playful toys and books and games
thank you for new shirt and pants and shoes
thank you for nourishing bread and beans and flour
thank you for warm cap and scarf and mittens
thank you for all the brown bags full of good things
thank you for all the brightly colored packages

thank you for all your good gifts cheering
thank you for all your loving hearts giving
thank you thank you thank you thank you
   from all the little ones in so many places
   who don't know your name or your face
   and yet bless you in his name

May his Word be heard to the ends of the earth
   in all the words to which we give speech
      be the sound of the God who sent us his Word

      hello welcome come in my home is your home
      I love you I care for you I cherish you
      may my God be your God my hope your hope
      may the merciful Lord be always with you
      go in peace and let's keep in touch
      when it is dark enough you can see the stars
      live today in fullness and tomorrow in hope

      may our speech be always yes yes no no

      yes to God when he tells us how to bear his Son
      yes to the Son when he calls us to follow him
      yes to the Spirit who brings us new life
      yes to the cries of all who need our help
      yes to keeping the beauty of all the earth
      yes to building God's new creation in love

      no to greed and excess and freakish lust
      no to blindness of mind and hardness of heart
      no to injustice and dishonesty and lies
      no to hatred and violence and war
      no to indifference and apathy and bitterness
      no to hunger and famine and starvation
      no to causing suffering and inflicting pain

In the beginning was the Word
   and the Word was with God
      and the Word was God

And the Word became flesh and dwelt among us

    and in this Word all our words are transformed
    all our words are made important but never final
    even the words spoken in anger or rejection
    even the words that wounded and hurt
    for there is no hurt so great no wound so deep
    that the Word cannot heal or reconcile given time
    for words can reach beyond time and space and death

    and the good news of Christmas
        is that God has come in our time and in our world
    and the Word become flesh in Mary
        and born in Bethlehem
    has hallowed our time and given power to our words
        and is born again in us this day
    for he has given us the power to become children of God
        as he was as he is as he will be
    and we have received him
        for he is grace upon grace gift upon gift
    to him be glory for ever and ever. Amen.

## The Family as Base Church

TIME: DECEMBER 31, 1989
SEASON: FEAST OF THE HOLY FAMILY
SCRIPTURE READINGS: SIRACH 3:2–6, 12–14;
  COLOSSIANS 3:12–21; MATTHEW 2:13–15, 19–23

A mother with several small, active children was having an especially bad day. Her husband was away, the washer broke down, the car battery was dead, and the children were going wild in the house because it was raining outside. Telling the neighbor the next day, she said: "It was an awful day. I even got a busy signal when I called Dial-a-Prayer, and when the call got through, I was put on hold."

I am sure many a mother, and many a father, can relate to this story. It may not be a typical day in the life of every family, but every day brings to every family a lot of pressures and minor crises, along with the occasional major ones. I am sure that in a community such as ours most families are two-career families, whose children are overachievers and involved in every kind of school and out-of-school activity, where time is the most precious commodity and priorities are most difficult to set because there are so many worthwhile choices.

And here I come, suggesting that the family should spend more time in shared prayer and ritual, in sharing faith and religious experience. I hope you don't hear what I have to say as one more burden, one more demand on your time, one more impossible dream from a celibate who has no idea what family life is all about. I only want to offer a suggestion about priorities and possibilities in family life today.

You have heard me repeat, and I hope you don't think I am beginning to sound like a broken record, that I feel the only hope for the vitality of the local church, the parish, and through the parish of the world church, is the development of small faith-sharing communities. I have been looking at a process named "Called to Be Church." It suggests three phases. In the first phase, eight to twelve people take time to communicate, to value each other, to belong to each other. Next they agree to support each other in a commitment to pray alone and to pray together. Finally, a small community develops confirming its identity in sharing the faith experience, in connecting with the church's story of faith, in reaching out to serve. This small community of faith becomes the base church.

Is this not what a family is supposed to be? Have you experienced this process, this unfolding reality, either in your family of origin or in your family of choice? Think about it for a moment. If you reflect on your experience as a member of a family, or as the creator of a family, I am sure you will discover how much of this process you have already lived through: learning to communicate, to value each other, deepening the sense of belonging to each other, encouraging one another to pray, both alone and together, developing connections to larger communities—a parish, a school, civic groups—reaching out to help others.

There is no doubt that the church looks upon the family in this light. The Christian tradition has long called the family the "domestic church," particularly since at the beginning of the Christian movement the believers did meet in each other's homes to share prayer, worship, teaching, and unity in faith and love. The National Catechetical Directory prepared by the National Conference of Catholic Bishops in the USA, titled *Sharing the Light of Faith*, puts it well: "The Christian family . . . [is] the basic community within which faith is nurtured" (221). There is your "base church," right in your own home.

This was exactly the situation of the family of Jesus. Jesus was born a Jew, and his family was a Jewish family. The evidence of the Gospels suggests that it was a devout family. From what we know of Jesus—and you can tell a lot about a family from the children—it was a family that followed the Jewish practice of teaching the Scriptures and religious values in the home, that observed feasts and rituals in the home, that prayed together at home, as all good Jews did then and continue to do to this day.

If you have had the occasion to become acquainted with an active Jewish family, especially one associated with the Orthodox tradition, I am sure you could not fail to admire the way their faith is part of their family life, the way the presence of God permeates their whole day, how they truly live in a covenant relationship with the Lord.

> The Jewish religion is very much a home-based religion. This has been a key to Jewish survival through the centuries, especially in times of persecution when worship at the temple or the synagogue was impossible. Some of the most important Jewish feasts and rituals are celebrated at home, including their greatest feast, Passover.[4]

The Catholic tradition has put more stress on our common worship at church, especially because the Eucharist is so central to our life. But the Church has also encouraged us to extend our celebrations and rituals to the home, in such ways as the use of Advent wreaths, nativity scenes, and a crucifix prominently displayed, marking a place of prayer during Lent. The faith we share here on Sunday, the prayer and worship for which we gather here today, depend to a large extent on the faith and prayer shared in the home during the week. This is not only for the sake of the children. As adults we learn at a deeper, more personally rooted level, what we practice and share with others. If you need some help in developing this dimension of prayer, ritual, faith-sharing in the family, the Bishops' Committee on the Liturgy has recently published a book titled *Catholic Household Blessings and Prayers,* containing a variety of blessings and prayers to be used in a family setting. In the introduction the bishops say:

> We hope that this book will find a place in every Catholic household—but not a place to rest. This book and the family Bible, side by side, should become worn out with use. Along with other signs—the cross, holy water, blessed candles—the presence of the Bible and this book expresses a way of life. This Catholic way—a way of daily justice, of service, and of care that is found around the family table and around the world's wide table—is our baptismal charge.... At the altar on Sunday, at table and bedside all week, we learn throughout our lives who we are: the body of Christ.[5]

From the base church of the family in the home, we gather here to build the local church, the parish family, and we are sent forth from here to build the world church, the human family.

## Who Shall Be Saved?

TIME: JANUARY 7, 1990
SEASON: FEAST OF THE EPIPHANY
SCRIPTURE READINGS: ISAIAH 60:1–6; EPHESIANS 3:2–6;
   MATTHEW 2:1–12

In ancient Egypt, the winter solstice was celebrated on January 6. It was celebrated as the appearance *(epiphaneia)* of the sun god; it was a feast of light, water, and wine. Possibly as early as the second century, Christians in the eastern part of the Mediterranean began to turn the feast into a celebration of Jesus' coming into the world, of his manifestation to the world as the Son of God. As you know, Greek Orthodox Christians and other Eastern Christians still celebrate the birth of the Savior on the Feast of the Epiphany, January 6.

There is much symbolism in this feast, many themes, many ideas expressed through symbol and metaphor. I would like to follow the symbol of light and see how it reveals the universal love of God. The light of the Lord is for all peoples.

Chapter 60 of the book of Isaiah comes from the third division of this work, the last to be written, from a time after the Israelites had begun to return from exile in Babylon. It is filled with hope and glory, the glory of the Lord who shines on the returning exiles. But this shining glory that breaks through the darkness and the thick clouds is not just for the Israelites. "The nations," the non-Jewish people, see this light and are able to walk by it. Kings admire the radiance of the Lord that shines on Jerusalem; they come from all parts of the world with caravans laden with gifts to Israel's God.

The Gospel of Matthew also presents the Lord as the light that guides the foreigners from the East to find the newborn "king of the Jews." The learned men from the East, with their wisdom about the heavens, have had their darkness pierced by a bright light. The star guides them on their journey, and from its place in the heavens points to the house where they find the child with Mary, his mother. The astrologers offer him homage and gifts. In Matthew's language they did him divine honors; they recognized the divine presence in him. The story for Matthew is not really about wise men from the East and their gifts; it is about Israel, the light to the pagans, shining to manifest God's glory. By the time this Gospel was written, many Gentiles were joining the original community of Jewish believers in Jesus, and the author wanted to show that this is the way things were intended by God to be from the very beginning.

The same message is proclaimed in the reading from Ephesians. Here it is the light of the manifold wisdom of God, it is the revelation of a secret plan, now being revealed. According to this plan, again, Gentiles and Jews are co-heirs, co-members, co-sharers of God's promises and gifts. What does this mean? It means that from the time of the ancient prophets, through the development of faith in Jesus Christ for the early Christians, and even to our time, the God of Israel, the God of Jesus Christ, our God, is not an exclusive God who favors one group of people and rejects others.

God's love is for all, without exceptions. The people whom God favors are chosen not for their own sake, for a privileged position, but for the sake of others—to serve them, to be the light that shines and leads others into the presence, into the mystery of God. Does that mean that everyone must come to believe as we do, that the whole world must become Christian? Not necessarily. We have seen a remarkable development in our thinking on this matter during the past fifty years or so.

Let's look for a moment at the question of the salvation of the Jews. The Council of Florence (1438–1445) declared that Jews were damned if they did not become Christians. Recently we have come to reflect anew and to understand better what Paul says in the Letter to the Romans: that all Israel will be saved. He states that even those Jews who reject the gospel of Jesus Christ are still by election the beloved of God for the sake of their ancestors, "for the gifts and call of God are irrevocable" (Rom. 11:29, 26–39).

Theologians today are proposing that perhaps the new covenant God made with us in Jesus Christ did not abrogate all the previous covenants, but went beyond them and added a new and ultimate dimension: the final, permanent, personal presence of God in Jesus Christ in the midst of his people, for the sake of the world. Theologians are beginning to suggest that perhaps Jews are "called to remain faithful to their own covenant, to maintain their extraordinary witness of faith, to contribute their own special insights and richness into the mystery of God."[6]

Does that mean that we stop evangelizing, that we stop proclaiming the Good News of Jesus Christ to others? Does that mean that it does not make any difference what anyone believes, that one religion is as good as another? Not at all. We believe that salvation has come to the world in Jesus Christ. We believe that we have a tremendous richness of truth, of experience, in our relationship with God, in religious history, and we want to share it with anyone who is interested in what we have to offer.

But we don't look down on, or dismiss, or condemn those who do not share our faith. God continues to reveal himself in creation, in history, in humanity, in ancient covenants, and in personal encounter. The salvation brought by Jesus to the world is now part of the very fabric of the world. It is at work everywhere, even where it is not explicitly recognized and accepted. We do not fully understand what God has done in Jesus Christ, and we never will. We leave the workings of his saving love to "the depths of the riches and wisdom and knowledge of God" (Rom. 11:33).

In the events of recent weeks in Eastern Europe [the collapse of many communist regimes] we are witnessing an extraordinary moment in history. I believe that we are seeing the salvation of God at work in our human history once again. I believe that God is revealing himself and his hidden, irrepressible work toward a new world, a new creation. I hope we don't see what is happening just as a triumph of the American way of life. I hope we don't expect the whole world simply to imitate and adopt our political system, our institutions, the ways of our capitalistic economy.

I hope that we may be open to learning, to discovering new possibilities. Perhaps there are new and unexpected ways to experience democratic freedoms, respect for the rights of every human being, opportunities for every nation and people and ethnic group to determine their human destiny and to share in the good things of the earth. Perhaps we can discover together new ways that diminish rather than increase the differences between rich and poor, that revalue the goods of the spirit and correct our seemingly insatiable appetite for material things.

Perhaps we can find ways to promote the common good while respecting the individual good of every person, ways that will unite us rather than isolate us, ways that will build the human family along with individual nations. I believe that these would be new ways of learning and proclaiming the meaning of Jesus Christ and of the salvation that he brought to the world.

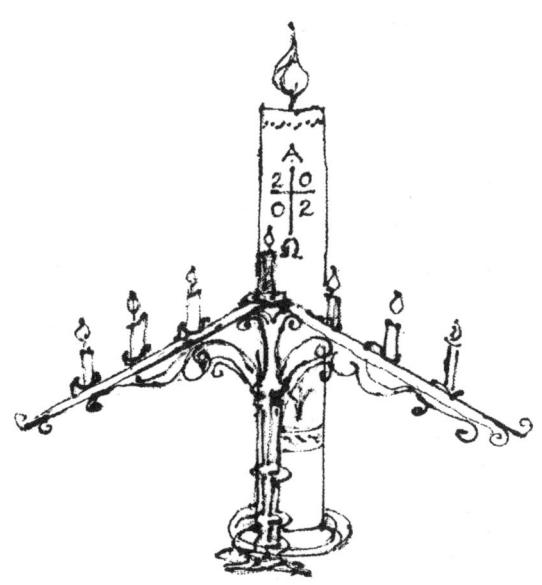

## The Meaning of Our Baptism

Time: January 10, 1993
Season: Baptism of the Lord
Scripture Readings: Isaiah 42:1–4, 6–7; Acts 10:34–38; Matthew 3:13–17

The biblical texts today complement each other in a marvelous way. The Gospel reading picks up the theme of the Isaiah song of the faithful servant, and the passage from Isaiah helps us to understand the event described in the Gospel. And in the second reading we have a witness from the early Christian community about what the baptism of Jesus meant to them: a turning point, the beginning of all that he did and said, the foundation for his mission, the sign that God's power was with him.

In our Gospel reading the voice speaks to the people gathered around John and presents Jesus to them as the Son of God: "This is my beloved Son. My favor rests on him." In Mark and Luke the divine voice speaks to Jesus personally: "You are my Son, my Beloved: you are my delight!" (Mark 1:11). For both Jesus and the disciples the baptism at the Jordan is an essential element for an understanding of the identity of Jesus. It tells us also who Jesus is and what he is called to be. Jesus is a first-century Jew; he belongs to this extraordinary people who for centuries had clung to their faith in one God, Creator and Lord of the universe, in the midst of tempting polytheistic religions with alluring practices and beliefs.

Jesus is there, in the midst of this people, when they are once again being called by the prophetic voice of John to make ready for a new coming into their midst of their demanding but loving, saving God. Jesus belongs to this people, and he himself has a unique, intimate, life-sharing connection with the God of Israel. The story of his baptism is one of the critical moments in the process by which the disciples came to recognize that Jesus was indeed the concrete, personal presence of the God who was coming into their history with salvation.

The language of the story also tells us how Jesus would accomplish his mission: He will be the faithful, suffering servant of Yahweh described by Isaiah five centuries before, wounded for our transgressions, who would carry the iniquity of us all. In the Gospel of Luke (4:16–21), in that powerful scene in the synagogue at Nazareth, Jesus reads another passage from Isaiah that describes the faithful servant and then proclaims: "Today this Scripture has been fulfilled in your hearing." There Jesus appropriates the mission of the servant as his own.

Here, in the story of his baptism, the language tells us that God has sent his beloved Son to be that faithful suffering servant: The opening of the sky, the symbolism of the dove, the words spoken are all clear references to that mysterious figure of the servant in Isaiah, powerful in his weakness, redeeming through his suffering, faithful unto death ,and vindicated by God in his power. That is the Jesus proclaimed by the Gospels.

How important is your baptism for your identity? Mine has become more and more important for me. A number of years ago I went looking for my baptismal certificate so that I could find the date and make the anniversary of my baptism a conscious remembrance, at least as important as my birthday. And when I go back to my hometown I have made it a habit to visit the cathedral and pray at the font where I was baptized. There are many other elements to my identity that define who I am, but I feel that everything else has been touched and modified by my baptism.

It was by my baptism that I became a member of the Christian people and of the Catholic Church, and in many ways I feel I have the same relationship to the Church that I have to my own family. The Church is my family in a very real sense, and it is part of me in a way that I could never deny or erase. There have been times when I have questioned why I continued to stay and work in the Church, but more than twenty years ago I came to the conclusion that I could never leave the Church: I loved her too much. I was willing to take the chance that the Church would ask me to leave, but I chose to stay.

I did want the Church to change, and I still do, in some fundamental ways, and I wanted to work for these changes. The only way I could do that was from within, not from the outside. I still find myself in disagreement with some of the official teachings and policies of the Church, but it is my Church, my family, my people, and it always will be.

For many, many years I thought that God had called me to be his servant. My understanding of what that means has changed tremendously from my seminary days until now. I grew up and received my seminary and original theological training before the winds of change and reform that were felt in the Second Vatican Council had begun to blow. When I was ordained I thought of the priest as a servant of God who exercised great power over the people for the purpose of bringing them to God. In a sense I was trained to serve God but also to lord it over the people.

It took me about ten years after ordination to realize that I did not have all the answers, that to serve God meant to serve his people, that the people of God had their own share of God's loving and saving power, that they had much to teach me. That's when I came to realize that the priesthood of the faithful, which we all share in baptism, comes first and is more significant than my sacramental, ordained priesthood. And it took another ten years or so before I came to understand that the ministry, the service of the people, your ministry and service, is where the kingdom of God is truly at work, and that the purpose of my ministry is to encourage and support and challenge you to be faithful servants of God in the world. That is what all of us are called to be by our baptism!

The most wonderful, beautiful, humbling, joy-filled realization of the meaning of my baptism came when, in a moment of prayer and meditation over the scene of the baptism of Jesus, I was suddenly struck by the feeling that in my baptism God was saying to me, as he said to Jesus, "You are my beloved son, you are my delight!" I am God's child, I am his joy and delight not because of what I do or accomplish, but because in his love he has made me his own. And the more I live in the consciousness of my baptism, the more I make that

moment long ago part of my life and being and identity right now, the more deeply I experience the power of this intimate relationship with God: He loves me as his dear child, his grace is with me, he takes delight in me.

Do you ever think about your baptism? Do you observe the day of your rebirth into the new life that God has shared with us in Jesus Christ? Do you feel the power of this decisive moment in your life when you were incorporated into God's holy people, made a member of that living organism that is the Mystical Body of Christ, called to be a faithful, self-giving servant of the Lord God of all creation, called by name to be a beloved daughter or son of the same God who is the Abba, the dear Father of Jesus, known by God with special joy and delight? That is what you are, all of that and more, by the grace of your baptism!

# Growing in Ordinary Time

TIME: JANUARY 14, 1996
SEASON: SECOND SUNDAY IN ORDINARY TIME
SCRIPTURE READINGS: ISAIAH 49:3, 5–6;
1 CORINTHIANS 1:1–3; JOHN 1:29–34

How are you doing with your new year's resolutions? Here we are, two weeks into the new year. How many of us still remember whatever it was that we resolved to do or to avoid doing during this year, in order to improve ourselves, to strengthen our relationships, to make ourselves better husbands or wives, better parents or children, better teachers or students, better professionals, or just better human beings?

The question I want to ask is this: What did we resolve to do to make ourselves better Christians, better followers of the Lord Jesus Christ? Have we been faithful in keeping these resolutions?

Being a good Christian, living a life faithful to our baptismal consecration in Christ Jesus, is not just a Christmas and Easter event, or a Sunday affair, or a string of words muttered under our breath as we shave or comb our hair or drive to work in the morning, or a quick "grace" rattled off in unison as we sit down to our evening meal. Being serious about our spiritual life, our union and communion with the Risen Christ, is not a task we can put off until we retire and have more free time. Being a good Christian, a faithful disciple of Jesus, is an every day and every hour and every minute, lifelong privilege and responsibility.

These questions and thoughts are suggested to me by the liturgical time we have just begun and by the Scripture readings for this Second Sunday in Ordinary Time. The biblical texts today speak to us of a critical moment in the life of Jesus, symbolized by his baptism at the Jordan River. The texts describe his moment of decision, the choice that Jesus made about how he would live his life and do the work the Father had given him to do. In the Gospel of John there is not a description of the event of the baptism, because in this Gospel the Jesus who speaks and acts is always very much the Risen Christ present and active in the believing community. There is no room in the Gospel for anything that would imply any imperfection or weakness or subordination in Jesus.

But the event of the baptism of Jesus in the Jordan was so critical that it could not be ignored, and the Gospel of John has all the language that we find in the story of the baptism of Jesus as told in the Synoptic Gospels of Matthew, Mark, and Luke, but without the actual event. John is baptizing, and the very reason he is baptizing with water is to give witness to Jesus. And that is what he does. He was told that the Spirit would come down on this unique individual. Now he has seen this, and the words that in the other three Gospels are spoken by the divine voice from the cloud become, in the Gospel of John, the testimony of John the Baptist, who says: "Now I have seen and testified that he is the Son of God."

The baptism was such a critical moment because it marked the beginning of Jesus' public ministry. The other texts today tell us how Jesus approached his mission and what he had resolved to do with his life. In the psalm we hear those powerful words of total commitment and obedience that the Letter to the Hebrews puts on the lips of Jesus: "To do your will, O my God, is my delight, and your law is within my heart!" (Ps. 40:9). In the passage from Isaiah we hear the choice that Jesus made about the form, the style that his ministry would take. He chose the model of the suffering servant of Isaiah. Jesus will be the faithful servant whom God will make a light to the nations, so that God's salvation may reach to the ends of the earth. In the last of the great poems on the suffering servant, Isaiah describes him as "a lamb that is led to the slaughter and a sheep that before his shearers is silent." This morning we heard John the Baptist point to Jesus and present him to the people with the words: "Here is the lamb of God who takes away the sin of the world!"

I hear today's liturgy as an invitation, as an urging to do with my life what Jesus did with his, to say, with Jesus, "to do your will, O my God, is my delight and your law is within my heart!" These should be our first words as we wake up in the morning, and the fundamental attitude that guides our life every day and every moment of the day. I hear today's liturgy as an exhortation to renew my commitment to the service of Jesus Christ and the gospel of salvation he came to proclaim. All of us, by our baptism, are called to be the faithful servants of God at all times, even if this means becoming the suffering servant at times.

To be serious about our spiritual life, our baptismal commitment, our deep yearning for a communion of love and an intimacy of being with God, we need discipline in our life, discipline in prayer, discipline in the effort to live a life of gospel simplicity, discipline in being open to the constant, living presence of the Lord in our heart and in every moment of our life.

My spiritual director died about a year and a half ago, and in the last two months I have begun a new phase of my spiritual journey with a new spiritual director. In a presentation to a group of priests about his approach to spiritual direction, my new director stated very clearly what he asks of anyone who comes to him for spiritual direction: every day, a half hour of meditative prayer, Mass, and some form of examination of life, and confession once a month. He expects this not just from priests and religious, but from everyone who comes to him for spiritual direction. For him, this is what is required to be serious about one's spiritual life. He does not demand this level of commitment from the start, but he expects everyone to be working toward this ideal. Because it is an ideal, no one will ever attain it perfectly, but it remains the ideal for the basic structure of our life of prayer and union with God.

At the beginning, I am firmly convinced that we need to make a commitment to some time and some form of quiet, listening, contemplative prayer at least three or four days a week, to participate in the liturgy of the Eucharist more than just once a week, to develop the habit of turning our thoughts and our feelings to God frequently during the day, to examine our life regularly to see both the good and the weaknesses and failures that are there, and to celebrate the sacrament of God's reconciling mercy at least every three or four months.

I know from experience that it is not easy to find a spiritual director, but I would still urge you to try to find someone who is willing to be a true spiritual friend, someone who is willing to be a companion to you on your spiritual journey.

Were any of these activities and attitudes part of your resolutions for the new year? It is not too late! A serious commitment to the spiritual life is not something reserved for people with special vocations or to special times of the year. It is for all of us, all of the time.

In the liturgy we have just begun what we call Ordinary Time. This is the most appropriate description for our life, is it not? There are peaks and valleys in every human life, moments of exalted ecstasy and dark despair, but is not most of our life just plain, ordinary time? And that is where we meet the saving mystery of our God, in the plain ordinariness of our life as parents and children, wives and husbands, teachers and students, in our homes, at our work or profession, in our volunteer activities, and in our neighborhood. Yes, we have the splendor of Christmas and Easter, we have those luminous moments of the celebrations of our first communion and confirmation and marriage and ordination, but most of the rest of our life is just plain, ordinary time.

The liturgical year of the Church has four weeks of Advent, two weeks for Christmas, six weeks of Lent, seven weeks of Easter, and thirty-three or thirty-four weeks of ordinary time. That means that two-thirds of the year is ordinary time. The Lord fills these ordinary days with his presence, and the Lord walks these ordinary roads by our side. We grow, or fail to grow, in our awareness of and obedience to and intimacy with the Lord mostly in the ordinariness of our life, because that is where we live most of our days. What are we doing about our ordinary spiritual growth, not just today, but tomorrow, and the next day, and the rest of the year?

# Working for the Kingdom

TIME: JANUARY 22, 1978
SEASON: THIRD SUNDAY IN ORDINARY TIME
SCRIPTURE READINGS: ISAIAH 8:23B–9:3;
   1 CORINTHIANS 1:10–13, 17; MATTHEW 4:12–23

If the first reading from Isaiah sounds familiar to you, it is because it is used as one of the readings for the Christmas liturgy. There the reference is to Jesus who comes as the great light to the people who walked in darkness. Today it is used in a very different way. It is part of the liturgy today because it is quoted in the passage of the Gospel of Matthew which we have just read.

This passage gives us Matthew's version of the beginning of Jesus' ministry. It follows immediately upon the story of the baptism of Jesus by the Baptist and the story of Jesus being tempted in the desert.

The three Synoptic Gospels—Mark, Matthew, and Luke—agree that Jesus began his preaching in Galilee, the northern part of Palestine. Matthew tries to explain why Jesus begins there, and he does it according to the purpose of his Gospel: to show that the Gentiles, the non-Jews, are included in God's plan of salvation from the very beginning.

Galilee was remembered as the ancient portion of the promised land given to the tribes of Zebulun and Naphtali. It was degraded because it took the brunt of all the invading armies from the north. As a result of frequent occupations it had acquired a mixed population, including many Gentiles. Isaiah proclaims that even for these people in their darkness the light of Yahweh will shine to dispel their gloom. Matthew sees that promise fulfilled in the presence of Jesus, who begins there the proclamation of the kingdom of God.

We are looking at Jesus as he begins to follow his vocation, to carry out his service, to be the faithful servant of Yahweh. He begins by calling people to repentance for the sake of the kingdom, by calling disciples to follow him and to abandon everything, by teaching and proclaiming the good news of God's salvation, and by making that salvation real, concrete, truly present, in the healing of illness.

Do you recognize yourself in the calling of Peter, Andrew, James, and John? Because they are called to leave everything and to follow Jesus, this scene has often been restricted to religious vocation and seen as applying to priests and sisters almost exclusively. And that is unfortunate, because it is really a calling of disciples, of followers. The special call to a group of twelve comes later. All of us are called first and foremost to be disciples, followers of Jesus, priests and sisters and lay people. The first vocation is discipleship, and only later is the disciple called to a specific form of service.

We are all called as Peter and Andrew, James and John were called. We are all called to let go of something in ourselves or in our possessions or in our surroundings, in order to follow Jesus. We cannot just remain the same and pretend to be serving the Lord. There has to be a change in our life if we hear his call and accept it. He cries out to us even today: "Reform your lives! The kingdom of God is at hand."

How do we answer God's personal call? What kind of change is demanded of us? I have a feeling that the most radical change in us will have to do not with some evil things that we must stop doing, but with the good that we have failed to do and must start doing. What must we do? What Jesus did.

Jesus did not invite Peter and Andrew, James and John to discipleship by giving them answers to all their questions about God. He invites them to share his journey, to join him in searching for ways to make the kingdom of God evident and real. Jesus is not the man with all the answers. He is not the Galilean whiz kid who amazes everybody with his remarkable knowledge of physics or psychology, or with his psychic powers to foretell the future. Jesus reveals God and his kingdom of justice and peace and love by interacting with people—by teaching them, healing them, loving them back to life. He points to the presence and action of God by reacting to the persons and events of daily life: a mother-in-law's fever, a child's need for affection, a blind man's longing for sight, a sinner's search for a friend. Matthew asks us to view Jesus as a prophet, as a man who wrestles with God by searching for a way to understand the persons and events that surround him. How can we do the same?

Can you recall all the persons whom you encountered last week and ask yourself: Was I to them a sign of the presence of God in their life, a sign of salvation? As a student, am I willing to go beyond the spirit of competition and share my knowledge and insights with another student to help him or her get a better grade? As a professor, am I willing to break through my isolation and take the time, make the effort, to listen to a student's problems, both human and academic, with sympathy and understanding? As a professional man or woman, do I try to meet whoever comes to ask me for my services not just as a client and a checkbook, but as a human being, with dignity and rights, feelings and needs? As a worker, do I make an effort to see and hear and meet my fellow workers, or my bosses, or those under me, as persons, and not just pieces of machinery or tools of the trade?

If we, like Jesus, are to become part of the fulfillment of the promise in the reading from Isaiah, we are called to bring light into the darkness and abundant joy and great rejoicing to our various life settings. We are called to help lift the yoke that burdens and the pole that ties the arms over the shoulders and binds in slavery. We are called to help break the whip of the oppressor. Perhaps it is the burden of a person going through a difficult divorce, or the paralyzing grief of someone who has lost a child. Perhaps we are called to take an active part in the liberation of the oppressed of our society: people of color, women, the elderly, the poor, homosexuals—yes, even homosexuals—and anyone else who for any reason might be denied his or her human rights and the opportunity to live in dignity and freedom.

We might need to listen to Paul's pleading in the letter to the Corinthians. If there are factions, divisions, hatreds, members of the same family who are not speaking to each other, people who speak words of peace but maintain enmity—in the academic community, in our parish community, in the greater community—then we are called as disciples of Jesus to work for unity and peace, to overcome divisions and heal wounds.

We are now in the Week of Prayer for Christian Unity. American churches have come a long way toward living with pluralism in theology, worship, and church life. Is this pluralism authentic brotherhood? Do we find genuine tolerance for and appreciation of differences within our communities, or would it be more honest to say that we are still divided? Should we rewrite the second reading and substitute different categories or different names to identify our divided allegiance, in the name of the Lord?

Like the first disciples, we are called to follow Jesus. We must learn, as they did, that following Jesus means taking on his view of the world and accepting his lifestyle. We are called to accept the kingdom of God in Jesus Christ and to be servants of that kingdom in our world, in all the many different situations in which we find ourselves.

## Choosing Poverty

TIME: JANUARY 29, 1978
SEASON: FOURTH SUNDAY IN ORDINARY TIME
SCRIPTURE READINGS: ZEPHANIAH 2:3, 3:12–13;
    1 CORINTHIANS 1:26–31; MATTHEW 5:1–12A

The Lenten season begins very early this year. I have a feeling that the meaning of this time of preparation for Easter has been increasingly lost, and that the observance of Lent in any significant way has disappeared almost entirely. The traditional motivations and obligations may have been faulty, but the opportunity for personal growth and for helping others offered by Lent is too vital and needed to let it go to waste. In preparation for Lent, we will take a fresh look at some old-fashioned ideas and practices in the hope of bringing them up to date, to see if they are still in some way appropriate for our time.

Today we hear words like humility, lowliness, meekness, weakness, poverty. How about these ideas for being old-fashioned—at a time when the national best-seller list has shown for 29 weeks the book *Looking Out for Number One*, which tells you how to go about getting all you can for yourself without much regard for others who may be competing with you.

The prophet Zephaniah spoke to an age of prosperity, when people felt that God was on their side because things were going well, and the pursuit of righteousness and justice took second place to the desire for material possessions. Zephaniah becomes a prophet of doom and warns the people of the imminent day of the Lord's anger. But he also speaks of a faithful remnant, made up of the humble and the poor, who in their need have retained a sense of their dependence on Yahweh.

Paul is writing to the Corinthians after receiving a report on the disorders, abuses, and errors that were threatening the existence of the community. One of the problems was people who regarded themselves as superior to others because of their knowledge of the Christian mystery. With bitter sarcasm, Paul reminds them that God has chosen the foolish and the weak and the lowly to confound the wise, the strong, and the proud.

The Gospel gives us the beginning of the Sermon on the Mountain, that disturbing instruction by Jesus to his disciples that seems to make such impossible demands on his followers and to turn upside down all the most cherished values of the world.

Are we the people humble and lowly? Are we the faithful poor waiting for deliverance? Are we the meek and the merciful and the peacemakers? As Americans, we are the envy of two-thirds of the world. We are citizens of one of the richest countries in the world, and our standard of living is the highest in history. We are six percent of the world's population, and we consume sixty percent of the world's protein.

As Americans, we may not be the wisest, but we certainly have the greatest access to education at all levels compared to any other people in the world, with all the possibilities that education makes available to us. We have access to more information and knowledge than any other population. That does not make us wise, but it makes available to us the tools or the raw materials that can be developed into wisdom.

As Americans, we exert enormous influence over the rest of the world, because of our military and economic power, because of the resources and technology we have developed. We are powerful!

As members of this community here at St. Paul Newman Center, we belong to the middle class or perhaps the upper middle class. The median household income in the United States in 1975 was $11,800. We are among the rich, the powerful, the well educated, and we are proud of our accomplishments and of our status.

Is that bad? Is it wrong to be rich? Only if our acquisition of wealth keeps others in poverty. Only if our overconsumption deprives others of what they need. Only if our preoccupation with material things blinds us to the deeper and greater realities—such as personal growth and the experience of a gracious and loving God, because we no longer feel the need of God—and makes us turn away from the needs of our brothers and sisters.

Does the teaching of Jesus demand that his disciples be materially poor and deprived and weak and powerless? Not according to the way Christian traditions have interpreted his teaching. That interpretation begins with the Gospel of Matthew, who probably added "in spirit" to the saying "Blessed are the poor."

Does the call to discipleship demand that we sell everything and give it to the poor in order to follow Jesus? There have always been individuals and groups who so interpreted and practiced the meaning of Christian discipleship. There are times when I feel personally that maybe that is what I should do, that the only authentic witness to the meaning of God's salvation in Jesus Christ is to be poor and to work with the poor. But I am not willing to make that decision and commitment, and so I cannot very well tell you that you should be poor and powerless in order to be a follower of Jesus.

We still need to develop a Christian theology out of the experience of the rich and abundant life. I believe that the rich and abundant life, in every sense, is the goal of creation, of evolution, of history, of individual life, of the vision and the lure of God toward creative development. But what is the role of Christian stewardship for those who have been called to live in the condition of richness and abundance?

I don't know the answer, but I have some tentative suggestions. I believe that we need to know the meaning of being poor, of having to go without things that are vital to our existence and that we take for granted, such as food, clothing, shelter. I believe this for several reasons.

First, we have gone beyond the necessities and turned them into luxuries. We live on rich food and throw 25 percent of our food into the garbage can. We have closets full of clothes that we no longer wear because they are not fashionable. We expect the most comfortable temperature in our home no matter what the season of the year. We need to learn the distinction between necessities and luxuries.

Second, we need to rediscover the relative importance of material things. They are not the reason for living. They are tools and means to other ends. There is more to life than physical satisfaction.

Third, we need to experience ourselves as persons in need—in need of each other, in need of God—to counteract the arrogance and self-sufficiency that makes us despise people in need and isolates us in our abundance.

Finally, we need to raise our consciousness and our sensitivity toward our brothers and sisters here and everywhere who are hungry, and cold, and desperately poor. Can we really know what it means to be hungry if we have never experienced hunger? Can we answer adequately the cry for help if we have never known the other person's pain?

If I had the time, I would like to develop this approach in reference to power and influence and pride. I want to say that we need to learn in our body, in our mind and heart, in our very being, the meaning of poverty, humility, meekness, lack of power. And I believe that the season of Lent is an urgent invitation and a present opportunity to do just that, to learn about hunger and thirst and being in need by our own free and voluntary choice, by our decision to live with less, to review our priorities, to reassess our values. And to do this not only for our own sake, but also for the sake of others.

Lenten sacrifice has meaning not in order to get us some gold stars on our heavenly report card, but to help us look at the meaning of our life here and now, to help us become free from our slavery to material things.

## Feast of Fools

TIME: FEBRUARY 9, 1975
SEASON: FIFTH SUNDAY IN ORDINARY TIME
SCRIPTURE READINGS: ISAIAH 58:7–10;
1 CORINTHIANS 2:1–5; MATTHEW 5:13–16[7]

If we read the newspapers every day and watch the news on television, we may find little cause for celebration and rejoicing. I think once in awhile we need to forget our troubles and let go of our fears and perhaps even of our caution, and celebrate all the beauty and the joy and the goodness that life still offers us. We need to do this not only as human beings but also as Christians and as members of an institution called the Roman Catholic Church. So this is our invitation to you today: to laugh and be happy and to rejoice, and perhaps even to be a bit foolish.

In the Middle Ages there was a day of celebration called the Feast of Fools, which was celebrated around the beginning of the year. On those days anything was allowed, and the humble people found all kinds of ways of making fun of the higher-ups. Lower-level clergy—perhaps even monsignors—put on gaudy masks and went around singing outrageous songs, even putting on the robes of bishops and cardinals and strutting around making fun of them. Mock kings and boy bishops were chosen from among the people. They ruled in outrageous ways. We have some echoes of this in the pranks of Halloween and the celebration of Mardi Gras.

Harvey Cox has a book entitled *The Feast of Fools,* in which he says that during this feast no custom or convention was immune to ridicule. Even the highest personages in the realm could be expected to be lampooned. You can see why this festival was never very popular with those in power. As a matter of fact, it was formally condemned by the Council of Basel in 1431. But it managed to survive up to the Protestant Reformation, and then it sort of disappeared. It is true that the Feast of Fools often degenerated into all kinds of excesses that were lewd and hurt people, but I think the loss of the idea is regrettable.

What I want to say today is that we need festival and fantasy. We need the ability to celebrate and to make a feast. We need the ability to laugh at ourselves, at our institutions, at our idiosyncrasies, and at all the silly little things that become so important and that we take so seriously in our lives. We need festival because human beings are creatures who not only work and think but also sing and dance and play and tell stories and celebrate. No matter what we have been brought up to think, work is not the purpose of life. Production, the accumulation of material possessions, always being busy, are not the reasons we were born.

Life itself is a goal, and to live fully and joyfully, to be alive, to enjoy, is the purpose of life. This applies even to our life as Christians and to our life in the Church. Sometimes we think that the Church is the goal of all our activities, or that ritual or worship or structures or authorities or titles or positions are the important things. They are not. It is the Christian life itself, more abundant life in Jesus Christ, that is the purpose of our being Christian. It is the kingdom of the Father that is described in the New Testament, in the Gospels, as a wedding feast, not a work detail. And it is a community of brothers and sisters—not a defense and protection of what we have staked out as our domain, not a defense and protection of our privileged position—a life in loving union and faithful service and welcoming openness. That's the goal of the Christian life.

We get a glimpse of this if we read the Acts of the Apostles and the descriptions of the early Christian assemblies where people came together in joy. We read that they were singing and sharing all that they had with one another. They were celebrating their being Christian in the Eucharist and the breaking of bread. In former times, and particularly in traditionally Catholic countries, the great festivals were Church festivals. There was a Christian dimension to festivity. I remember that when I was growing up the biggest celebration in our town was the feast of our patron saint. That was the big fair. The whole square was filled with rides and games and shooting galleries and circus games—and even that terribly wicked institution that was severely chastised by the Church, which we were forbidden to even walk by: the dance pavilion.

You know the ingredients of festival. Food and drink and games and play and dancing and singing and friends and family and all kinds of people to share the joy in a carefree and happy attitude that allows us to enjoy all that is good in the moment. There is time enough to worry about the future and to be responsible about our duties. Is this attitude un-Christian? Of course it can be, but it does not have to be, because it can also be a celebration of our consciousness of the gifts of God's love, a celebration of all that God has done for us in the past, by memory, and of all that God has promised for the future, in hope—a celebration that arises from a profound attitude of faith.

In our own perspective we need fantasy. We need to be able to imagine. We need to be able to construct new worlds and different ways of seeing and of living. If we are unable to do that, how can we escape from the drudgery and the hopelessness and the gloom of daily life? If we are unable to imagine, to construct in our fantasy a new and different world, how can we ever go about making it happen? We need fantasy to express our understanding of reality in a manner that is alive, that is vivid, that is gripping. We need myths. We need to develop myths for our understanding because life is too rich, too varied, too mysterious to be simply boxed in and encased in words and ideas and abstractions, in plans and policies and budgets and other sensible, practical things. These practical things are needed, but we must know that they are not all there is to life.

We need imagination and fantasy so that we will have poetry and music and painting. Without fantasy and imagination, we would never have the words that move us deeply and profoundly. We would never sit and listen to a piece of music that brings us peace or excitement or joy. We need fantasy, we need imagination, to make fun of ourselves and our experiences, to make fun of the powerful in our midst. Yes, we should make fun even of our ecclesiastical superiors. We should be able to laugh at some of the silly things that we still do—like the bishop wearing a little skull cap on his head. This custom originated when bishops shaved their heads and needed to cover them to keep them warm in the unheated palaces of Rome. In Italian this cap is called a *zucchetto*, which means little pumpkin! We should be able to laugh and make fun of the way newly elected bishops even today, in all seriousness and pomp, will engage somebody to draw a coat of arms for them as if being elected to the bishopric really made them members of the nobility—which doesn't exist anyway—and gave them all the titles and privileges of a feudal lord as if the system had not died five centuries ago.

Jesus reminded his disciples that there was a time to feast and a time to fast. The time to fast begins this coming Wednesday. Today is a time to feast. Paul tells us that we should be willing to be called fools for the sake of Christ. Maybe all the careful prudence, the prudence of all the worldly ways we have developed to survive, is not exactly the way we are called to live as Christians. We have a great deal to celebrate. We are alive. We are human, with all the marvelous things that implies. We can see and we can hear, we can speak and we can sing, and we have one another and the love of the Father, the presence of the Son, and the gifts of the Spirit. Paul puts it very well:

> Do not deceive yourselves. If you think that you are wise in this age, you should become fools so that you may become wise. For the wisdom of this world is foolishness with God. . . . So let no one boast about human leaders. For all things are yours, whether Paul or Apollos or Cephas or the world or life or death or the present or the future—all belong to you, and you belong to Christ, and Christ belongs to God. (1 Cor. 3:18–23)

If that is not adequate reason for rejoicing and celebration, then I don't know any other reason. May God bless us.

## Facing Temptation

TIME: MARCH 4, 1990
SEASON: FIRST SUNDAY OF LENT
SCRIPTURE READINGS: GENESIS 2:7–9, 3:1–7;
  ROMANS 5:12–19; MATTHEW 4:1–11

Both the reading from Genesis and the one from the Gospel of Matthew are "narrative theology" rather than descriptions of actual events. They are theological interpretations of fundamental mysteries in human life and history, interpretations based on profound faith experiences. As you probably know, there are two stories of creation in the first three chapters of Genesis. The first one organizes creation in the process of seven days. It concludes with the glory of man and woman created in the image and likeness of God—after which God rested in the contemplation of the goodness of his work. The second story begins: "In the day the Lord made the earth and the heavens, . . . the Lord God formed man of dust from the ground . . ." (Gen. 2:4b–7). This story ends with the sin and fall of the first man and woman and their exile from the garden of delights.

The second creation story was written during the glorious days of the monarchy of David and Solomon, a time of national pride and optimism—a time to retell the stories of the people, to go back in imagination to the very beginning of things, to show how Yahweh God's choice and guidance had been there from the beginning. But even in the best of times there is injustice and suffering, pain and loss, and death. How can we account for the evil we experience? In the Hebrew view evil could not come from God, so it had to come from something the first human beings had done wrong, something that touched and involved the whole human race. Hence the now-familiar story of the fall.

There is evil in the world that we are unable to explain, but there is also a lot of evil that is the result of our wrong choices and bad decisions, of our greed and selfishness, of our pride and lust, of our sinfulness. This is true both in a historical sense and in a personal sense. You and I personally have made wrong, sinful decisions that have resulted in isolation and alienation, pain and suffering for ourselves and others, broken relationships with God, with others, with ourselves.

For Paul, what happened in Adam is totally reversed in Christ. Death was the consequence of sin. The fact that all die is proof that all men and women sin, but the overflowing grace of Jesus Christ has overcome our sinfulness. In his resurrection, even death is conquered.

We can see this reversal in the story of the temptation of Jesus as told by Matthew. The setting is different: not a lush garden, but a barren desert. The actors are similar: Jesus, like Adam, is the one in whom humanity is summed up; the tempter has a different form but is really the same deceiver as the serpent. The temptation is similar: to seek one's own glory, to use power for oneself. But the choice is different. Jesus makes his decision for God, not for his own convenience. He refuses to force God to ratify and justify his ambition. In everything he puts God first, not himself.

To say that this is theological narrative rather than actual event is not to say that Jesus did not face these choices. He did, throughout his public ministry. He could have used his power to develop a political following, an earthly domain. How many times people came looking for him because he had cured people, freed people from their demons, fed the multitudes. They wanted to follow him because of his power. They wanted him to lead them, to lead Israel to new success and glory. They wanted to make him king. Would he not be a good and strong and wise king like David and Solomon? Is he not their descendant? But Jesus hides from them, because that is not the way he understands the mission he has received from the Father. He is called to be the faithful, suffering servant, not the triumphant king.

How many times leaders and people asked Jesus for a sign. Do something extraordinary, they demanded, like flying off the top parapet of the temple, something spectacular that will show us that God is on your side, and we will believe in you. And that last bitter taunt, that last tempting invitation: If you are the Son of God, come down from that cross! Save yourself, and we will believe you!

We know what choices Jesus made. Do we know how much these choices cost him? I don't think anyone can really know that. We can see the external consequences: the opposition of the leaders and eventually of the crowd, the misunderstanding and abandonment by his friends, the anguished agony in the garden, the unfair trial, the mocking of the soldiers, the scourging, the crushing weight of the cross, the desperate cry: "My God, my God, why have you forsaken me?," the death on the cross.

But we don't know the questions and doubts that went on in the mind and heart of Jesus, the agony of making the decision, the uncertainty about whether it was the right decision when everything seemed to fail. We don't know the fear and the pain and the darkness and the hopelessness in the mind of Jesus. Why couldn't he have saved his people by being a strong and wise king? Why couldn't he have had the admiration and adoration of the people, instead of their hatred and scorn? Why couldn't he have given praise to God as the high priest in the splendor of the temple, entering the Holy of Holies amidst the clouds of incense to sprinkle the blood of animals, instead of climbing the altar of the cross and pouring out his own blood?

Because, for some mysterious reason that neither Jesus then nor we now fully understand, the only triumph that is really worthwhile, the only victory that is really final, the only glory that truly lasts, is the triumph that comes through the crucible of suffering, the victory that comes through the agony of defeat, the glory that arises from the shame of the cross.

I firmly believe that this is the mystery that we are preparing to celebrate at Easter, the mystery that we are called to live every day of our life by the fact of our baptism: The story of the resurrection for Jesus comes only after the pain and the shame of the cross. And I firmly believe that the same is true for us. New, risen life comes only after the experience of pain and death. Do you believe this? Does your experience suggest to you that this is true, that by the power of God suffering can be changed into deeper and greater joy, that loss can be changed into gain, that death can be transformed into life?

This is the challenge of the Christian life that is presented to us once again in this season of Lent. Are we willing to follow Jesus into the darkness so that we can share his light? Are we willing to chose the way of the suffering servant with him for the sake of the victory of God's redeeming love in ourselves and in the world? Are we willing to pick up our cross daily and follow Jesus in his death so that we can share in his risen life?

As difficult as this choice may seem, I don't know of any other choice that will bring us the depth of peace, the fullness of life, for which our hearts yearn. Nothing else: no fruit of forbidden tree, no drugs, no sex, no power, no fame, no money. Only God, the loving God to whom Jesus was faithful through all his temptations, through all his life. Him alone do we adore; to him alone do we give honor and glory.

## Coming Down from the Mountaintop

Time: March 11, 1990
Season: Second Sunday of Lent
Scripture Readings: Genesis 12:1–4a; 2 Timothy 1:8b–10; Matthew 17:1–9

Have you ever been to a mountaintop? I have. When I was young I used to go mountain climbing. Now I ride ski lifts that take me to the tops of many mountains. It is an extraordinary experience to have climbed to the top of a mountain. The total silence, the clear air that allows you to see incredible distances, the stunning grandeur of the mountains, seeing yourself in scale against this immense scene—all are unforgettable experiences. For me, they are often deeply moving religious experiences. In mountain climbing, having to leave and climb down always seems more difficult than the ascent. In skiing I like to go to the top of the mountain before the last run to stop and, in silence, take in as much as I can of the magnificent view.

Maybe that is what happened at the top of the mountain of transfiguration. The dramatic story we heard in the passage from the Gospel of Matthew may be the writer's attempt to describe an intense moment of union with God in prayer that was experienced by Jesus and witnessed by some of the disciples. This section of the Gospel is a key point where several things come together. It is a reaffirmation of the identity of Jesus, an anticipation of the glory of the resurrection and the Parousia, a moment of joy and comfort in the midst of brooding thoughts about suffering and death.

The story of the transfiguration in the Gospels is framed between the first and second predictions of the passion, death, and resurrection. Jesus is becoming more conscious of the fate that awaits him, and he wants to warn his disciples, to let them know that they, too, must be willing to take up their cross if they want to follow him, to let go of their life if they want to truly and finally possess it.

It is only natural to want to avoid the cross, to want to stay where it is safe and comfortable. Peter, in the scene described in the chapter that precedes today's reading, tries to argue with Jesus about what he said about his capture and passion and death. In today's moment of glory, Peter doesn't want to leave. He wants to build a little shelter and just stay there. Jesus, in the garden on the night before he died, asks that he be spared the cup of suffering, the death on the cross, if at all possible.

But it is not always possible to avoid the cross. Sooner or later we have to come down from the mountaintop. All of us, sooner or later, in one way or another, will be faced with the reality of pain, suffering, loss, death. It comes with the territory of our limitations and weakness, of the imperfect material world in which we live, where accidents happen and things break down and our life energies begin to diminish.

The phone will ring in the middle of the night, and our life will never be the same again. The doctor will tell us he has bad news. Some pain will make its presence felt and never leave. The job we wanted will be given to somebody else. The person we love so desperately does not love us. We look into the face of unbearable pain in another, and there is nothing we can do except be there and share it.

What are we going to do with our cross? It is not enough to say that we have to carry it because there is no other choice. Somehow we have to learn to embrace it, to accept it as Jesus did, as part of a greater reality, a greater purpose—however difficult it may be to understand that purpose. To accept, as Jesus did, with a sense of loving surrender to the one who has the power to rescue us. To accept with the same sense of giving ourselves into the hands of the one whose love will save us and keep us from the abyss of darkness and despair.

The first step in our movement from cross to crown, from pain to gain, is this trusting faith and loving surrender to the God who will not abandon us, who will never let us go, who will not let us perish, who will transform us and change our suffering into gladness. It is the experience at the top of the mountain that tells us this. In Jesus Christ we are God's beloved sons and daughters, and God will come to us as he

came to Jesus. Paul tells us in today's reading from Timothy that, in Christ, "God has robbed death of its power and brought life and immortality into clear light through the gospel."

But there is another dimension to the reality of pain and suffering, and that is its redemptive power. The cross has the power to save, to transform, to make things different. Not only the cross of Christ, but our crosses as well. In another passage Paul declares: "I rejoice in my sufferings for your sake, and in my flesh I complete what is lacking in Christ's afflictions for the sake of his body, that is the Church" (Col. 1:24). What happened in the physical body of Christ can happen in us, his disciples, for we are his mystical body, the continuation of his concrete, historical, physical presence in the world.

The most powerful image of redemptive suffering is the figure of the suffering servant in Isaiah. This was Jesus' choice for his own ministry, and it was perhaps the first title given to him by the disciples after his resurrection. The suffering servant is not someone who endures passively the consequences of self-centered and destructive power. The suffering servant, Jesus, is one who can sustain a loving relationship even in the face of hate; who can take in and hold the indifference and the hatred of the other without breaking the relationship; who continues to respond with love for the other, and so continues to maintain the possibility of love in the other as well.

Redemptive suffering is all the energies for good that are released in the face of evil, in the experience of suffering. Redemptive suffering is the commitment to justice not only for ourselves but for everyone that arises from the experience of personal injustice. Redemptive suffering is the power to continue loving until even hate is transformed into love. Redemptive suffering is the ability to endure hardships until they are transformed into grace for ourselves and for others. Redemptive suffering is the willingness to endure even death for the sake of new life. This is what happens when God shares our suffering in Jesus Christ. This is what can happen when we are willing to take up our cross and follow Jesus. This is how the cross is transfigured into glory.

## Women Priests?

TIME: MARCH 14, 1993
SEASON: THIRD SUNDAY OF LENT
SCRIPTURE READINGS: EXODUS 17:3–7; ROMANS 5:1–2, 5–8; JOHN 4:5–42

Today's Gospel is one of the most dramatic stories about Jesus. Have you been reading the series in *The Fresno Bee* on "Megatrends for Women"? On Monday, there was an article entitled "A new era emerges as women defy religious traditions." In it Sister Sandra Schneiders, a highly respected biblical scholar from Graduate Theological Union in Berkeley, makes reference to the Samaritan woman as the only person, besides John the Baptist, who preached the gospel during Jesus' public life. "But, she concludes, tradition merely wrote this woman off as someone who had five husbands."[8]

The story of the Samaritan woman is one of the key biblical passages for the women's movement in the Church, but it is much more than that. It is a powerful, magnificent lesson in human, and particularly male/female, relationships. And much more.

First let me set the stage so that we understand the historical situation. In the Gospel of John, Jesus goes to Jerusalem at least three times. Today's story takes place after his first visit to Jerusalem, as Jesus is making his way back north to Galilee. To do this he had to cross Samaria. For the Jews, the Samaritans were heretics, traitors, despised half-breeds, and enemies. Jews would have nothing to do with Samaritans. The situation was very similar to what we see happening today in Croatia and Bosnia.

Another important element of the story is that the social conventions of the time prevented a man from talking in public to a woman who was not a member of his family. A rabbi never spoke to any woman in public, and women were not allowed to study the law as disciples of a rabbi. The woman in the story may also have been a social outcast, because of her marital situation. The fact that she comes to the well in the middle of the day, rather than in the morning with all the other women, may be because she was shunned by them. The scene is set then for a confrontation between two strangers, enemies even, coming face to face in a very difficult, uncomfortable situation.

What happens? The encounter begins with some testiness and sharp words, some argumentative questions about each other's background and traditions. But we also see an amazing openness, we witness a growth in mutual understanding and acceptance, to a level of trust, of giving and accepting responsibility that fly in the face of all social conventions and break through the barriers of separation and the bonds that kept women in an inferior, dependent condition.

Jesus begins by sitting on the well. Showing his tiredness, he reveals his need. He is thirsty, and he asks for a drink of water. He gives the woman the opportunity to be a gift to him. As the conversation continues, Jesus also has a gift to offer the woman, and she reveals her needs and desires. He does not judge her or condemn her but draws her out and leads her to astonishing insights into his identity and mission. The woman first calls Jesus a Jew, a term of contempt. Next she addresses him with respect, and calls him Sir. Then she begins to sense a special power in him and calls him a prophet. Finally, she recognizes that he is the one sent by God and describes him as the Messiah.

The entire dialogue and encounter is suffused with growing mutual respect and honesty, with mutual challenge but also with compassion. Jesus is patient and kind, and he accepts the woman as she is. The woman is open and willing to ask questions about Jesus' identity. She is more honest in her questions than even the disciples. An encounter that begins with suspicion, distance, and argument ends in mutual respect and acceptance.

And then the most amazing thing happens. Jesus chooses the woman to take on the role of an apostle, to go and announce the good news of salvation to her town. And she is willing to take the risk—to go to the people who probably had condemned her and avoided contact with her because of her past, and to invite them to the life-giving waters that Jesus had offered to her. And, incredibly, the town listens to what she has to say. The people come to Jesus because of her story, and many come to believe in Jesus as the Savior of the world.

What power is in this story! Jesus breaks through all the social, ethnic, political, religious barriers of his time and treats the woman at the well as an equal, as a full person. In his time he would have been regarded as a radical feminist! (Of course, there was no such word or concept in his time.) The encounter leads to the experience of a personal relationship that has all the qualities our human relationships need to be life-giving and supportive, to make life rich and worth living. I think this is the deepest and most desperate thirst we have today, the thirst for someone to love and for someone to love us in return. We yearn for human relationships that are positive and enriching, based on mutual respect and understanding, mutual acceptance and openness, mutual vulnerability and support.

Do you hear what the story of the woman at the well is saying to us today? Do you hear what it says about the way Jesus feels and acts and reaches out and gently challenges us today to open ourselves to him, to his love and to the love of his Father? Do you hear what the Gospel is telling us about our human relationships, especially our female/male relationships?

Jesus shatters the accepted customs of his society to treat the Samaritan woman with respect, as an equal, capable of being both a disciple and an apostle in the fullest sense of the word. There is no struggle for power in the story, no attempt by one to use the other, no demeaning behavior. And this is not Jesus acting as the Eternal Word of God, as the Risen Lord of all, which is the way Jesus is portrayed most of the time in the Gospel of John. This scene is not one of the great signs that in John manifest the power of God present in Jesus. This is one of the few instances when we see a very human Jesus, who is tired and thirsty, who needs someone to give him a drink, who is willing to take the risk of breaking the social conventions and even raising the eyebrows of his disciples.

Do you hear what the Gospel story of the Samaritan woman has to say to the Church today? Are we willing to see Jesus as someone who would ignore the constraints of religious respectability? If he were here today, would Jesus ordain women to the priesthood? I believe he would. I believe that Jesus would empower every woman, just as he would empower every man, to be a disciple and apostle, to proclaim the gospel of salvation and to celebrate the signs of his presence and love in our midst. Although priestly ordination is not the only way to do ministry for the sake of God's kingdom, if priestly ordination were necessary to proclaim the equality of women and men as disciples and ministers of God's grace, I believe that Jesus would ordain women to the priesthood.

## Living with the Mystery

TIME: MARCH 29, 1981
SEASON: FOURTH SUNDAY OF LENT
SCRIPTURE READINGS: 1 SAMUEL 16:1B, 6–7, 10–13A; EPHESIANS 5:8–14; JOHN 9:1–41

Do you ever feel that the closer you draw to any person the more you realize how little you know about him or her, that the more we know about a person the more we realize the complexity, the mysteriousness of the human personality, of human freedom, of the constantly changing process that each of us is?

A recently married college student was assigned to write an essay for one of her classes about the person she loved most. She found it very difficult to put into words the reality of her husband. Finally, in a moment of insight, she decided to write about him as a mystery, whom even she could not completely understand. But you don't have to understand love. We are learning more and more to recognize and to respect the dimension of mystery in humans, in nature, in everything that is. Have we learned to respect the mystery of God?

In the traditional Latin liturgy, the position of the priest and the people all facing toward the altar seemed to point to a mysterious reality out there, to the transcendent, infinite God in heaven. The new liturgy looks to the community. We look at each other, we speak to each other, you can hear and understand every word I speak. Has this destroyed our sense of mystery? It has certainly shifted its focus. It forces us to look beyond the external signs of mystery to the more hidden reality of God. The liturgy today points to God among his people—to the immanent, close-at-hand God. Perhaps with God, as with each other, the closer we become, the more we are confronted with the mystery of the other.

In the first reading, Samuel is surprised. Why does God choose David? He seems such an unlikely choice, a young boy to lead the people in times of national calamity. This is one of the most difficult aspects of God's mystery: his choices. Why

David? Why me? Moses, the prophets, the disciples in today's Gospel. Why is this man born blind? Have you ever asked this question of God? Why me? What kind of answer did you get?

There is a tendency to develop our own answers, our own ways of coping with mystery. We try to domesticate the mystery of God, to make him fit into the walls of our homes, into the limits of our minds. The Hebrews had made a tremendous discovery about their God: He was holy, three times holy, different from other gods, from the ways of his people, set apart, living at a distance, not like what happens every day. Then, in the course of their history, they began to apply the word "holy" to the place where God dwelt, the temple, to those who ministered to God in the temple, to the objects used in worship, to the books that recorded God's history with his people. It was almost as if through all this they could manage this tremendous mystery, they could deal with it, would know what to expect.

But just as the Hebrews seem to know what to expect, God shatters all their expectations and comes into their midst as an ordinary human being, as one of them. No wonder they had such a difficult time understanding Jesus, seeing him for what he was. Some of the leaders could look at Jesus and see in him only the Sabbath breaker, the one who by his very presence called into question their cherished ideas about God. It is the man who is not learned in the law, the man who receives the unexpected gift of sight, who is willing to find out who this person is who has enabled him to see. It is this man who comes to the insight that is all-important, who recognizes and worships God's presence in this man Jesus.

There is a profound difference between blindness and the acceptance of mystery. Blindness in today's Gospel is thinking that we know it all when in fact we are not even aware that we do not know; thinking that we have the answer to all mysteries when in effect we have only the answers we have made up ourselves; thinking that we see the universe when in fact we see only the four walls we have built around ourselves. Acceptance of mystery means knowing the limits of our ability to know and understand, respecting the question that has no answer, accepting the presence we do not understand fully.

Think of the dramatic story in today's Gospel, the dialogue between the cured blind man and the leaders. The leaders are sure that they are not to be counted among the blind. The blind man who now can see asks: Who are you, that I may believe in you? And then: I do believe, Lord.

What does it mean for us to accept the mystery of God in Christ? First, it means to be mindful, always, of the limits of our knowledge and faith; never to pretend that we know God and Jesus fully; never to impose the limits of our knowledge and our loving on God; never to say "God cannot do that," because God will surprise us. It means never to presume to know who God saves and who he does not save, or how God saves. It means never to speak of God in either/or terms. God is both/and: just and merciful; near and far; self-revealing yet hidden in mystery; willing to work through us and through human history yet always greater than anything humans can imagine, unable to be contained by any human institution, not even by the Church.

Accepting the mystery of God in Christ means we must be open to the unexpected, ready for the moment of novelty, ready and open to the mysterious ways in which Gods reaches us, touches us, reveals himself to us: in brilliant sunshine, in gentle rain, in the breathtaking majesty of a mountain, in the delicacy of a flower, in the smile of a child, in a moment of pain, in the peace of a dying friend. God escapes all our attempts to control him, to manipulate him, to make him behave according to our rules: He is free; he has the greatness to encompass all possibilities; he is holy.

Accepting the mystery of God in Christ means that we confess Jesus as Lord not because we can prove him to be God by miracles performed or prophecies fulfilled, but because he has called us by name and we have met him in faith and found in him a love, a mercy, a compassion, a strength, a faithfulness, a self-giving, a patience in the face of death, and a victory over death that leads us to accept and confess that he is truly man and truly God.

The mystery of God in Jesus Christ, already present with us because we have gathered in his name, already proclaimed in the holy word of Scripture, will soon be expressed in a personal way in the sacramental signs of the Eucharist. Let us approach our eucharistic communion today with a profound sense of the tremendous holiness of God made present in our midst, with the most intense sense of reverence and gratitude and joy that the mystery of God comes to us in bread and wine.

# The Cruise Ship of Life

TIME: APRIL 5, 1987
SEASON: FIFTH SUNDAY OF LENT
SCRIPTURE READINGS: EZEKIEL 37:12–14;
ROMANS 8:8 –11; JOHN 11:1–45

I am sure many of you know about or have seen book by Charles Schulz, *The Gospel According to Peanuts*. Certainly most of you are familiar with the "Peanuts" cartoon strip, which often raises some serious questions about life and the way we live it. In one strip, Lucy describes life as a cruise ship. She tells Charlie Brown that on the cruise ship of life people have these big canvas chairs. Some take their chairs to the back of the ship to recall the memories of a life already lived, while others place their chairs on the bow of the ship to look forward and dream of a life yet to come. Then Lucy asks: "Where do you take your chair, Charlie Brown?" He answers: "My problem is that I don't know how to open my chair."

Where do we find ourselves in the story of the resuscitation of Lazarus? Do we identify with any of the characters of the story? Who are we? The disciples, who are close to Jesus, but still do not understand what he is about? Martha, who is angry because Jesus did not come to heal her brother, and who still expects a miracle to give her back her brother? The Jews, who now are willing to believe because they have seen the sign? Are any of us willing to identify with Lazarus, to recognize that in some ways we are dead, to grapple with the fear in the depth of our heart, that maybe it is too late for us? The whole point of the Gospel story is that it is never too late when Jesus is present, when we believe that he is resurrection and life.

There are exceptions, I know, but generally we have such a strong desire to live that we cling to life desperately. We think of Jonathan Clark, a baby who needs a liver transplant and is fighting for his life, who evokes such sympathy and unites thousands of people from all religious backgrounds into a community of prayer for his recovery. Perhaps we should also unite in prayer for all the lives that are terminated in the womb through abortion and never are born, and for all the people who contemplate such tragic decisions.

But are we really alive? Do we really live, or do we just go through the motions? Lazarus is a symbol of every man and woman who is bound by any form of living death: depression caused by loss, anxiety about the future, paralyzing fear, numbing dependence, the sick person uncertain of recovery, the professional who discovers there is no satisfaction in his or her work, people facing the possibility that a marriage or other relationship has disintegrated, parents enduring the agony of a child's trouble or destructive behavior, the widow or widower trying to adjust to living alone, the adolescent struggling to find meaning in life and reasons for hope, the person growing old and facing the loss of choices and dignity. Perhaps, in some way, we are all Lazarus. We all need to hear the Lord call out to us: "Come out of your tomb, so that you may be set free!" He is the only one who can bridge spirit and matter, life and death, present and future, human and divine life.

When Jesus calls us, if we answer his call, what we experience should not be just a resuscitation, a going back to the same life we were living before. That is what happened to Lazarus. We are called to share in the new life of the resurrection. We are called to participate in the mystery of the divine life here and now, without waiting for bodily death. This is the constant theme of the Gospel of John: If we are alive, and if we believe in Jesus, we will never die, because eternal life is already in us, because we already share the intimate, life-giving union of Father and Son.

If we really believe in Jesus as the eternal Word of God made flesh for our salvation, if we believe that he is the resurrection and the life for us and for the whole world, then we have a new life, not just the old one given back. We are a new creation. This is what we are preparing to celebrate on Easter. Having struggled during Lent to develop a new level of self-discipline, having struggled with our addictions of all sorts, with all the things that enslave us, having tried to give our best time and concentration to the Lord in prayer and silence, having chosen to give ourselves to the Lord each day, morning and evening, all that we are and all that we do, having discovered that if we really give ourselves to the Lord we end up being more available to the needs and the hurts of our brothers and sisters, we cannot just go back to what we were before Lent. If we have put this sincere effort into our spiritual growth during Lent, we must be different and continue to live a different life, a life of deep faith in Jesus, a life of unshakable hope in his promises, a life of sincere love for the Lord and for one another.

On this fifth Sunday of Lent, our catechumens come forward for their final scrutiny. We will pray: "Lord Jesus, you raised Lazarus from death as a sign that you had come to give us life in the fullest measure. . . . By your Holy Spirit, fill them with life. . . ."

Our catechumens' careful examination and final preparation and purification for full initiation at Easter invites all of us to re-evaluate how we live, to notice where we have placed our priorities, where we have set up our deck chairs. While we do not forget the past or stop dreaming of the future, our focus is on the present. Now is the time to live that fuller, more abundant life in Jesus Christ. Now is the time to share that life with the world—even, or especially, because we still face the specter of nuclear war, hunger and poverty, injustice and violence. Like Martha and Mary, we need both to hear and to proclaim that the Lord is here, and that he is the resurrection and the life. Do we really believe? Can we answer joyfully with Martha: "Yes, Lord, I believe that you are the Messiah, the Son of God, the one coming into the world"?

## Giving Thanks for the Eucharist

TIME: APRIL 16, 1987
SEASON: HOLY THURSDAY
SCRIPTURE READINGS: EXODUS 12:1–8, 11–14;
1 CORINTHIANS 11:23–26; JOHN 13:1–15

Earlier this week, as Jewish families throughout the world sat down to the Seder on the first night of their celebration of Passover, a ritual question was asked: "Why is this night different from all other nights?" We hear this question repeated in our readings here this evening, because this night for us is different from all other nights.

Why is this Eucharist different from all other celebrations of the Eucharist? Because we recall directly the historical moment of the Lord, the night when Jesus sat at table with his disciples and for the first time broke the bread and shared the cup as the sacrament of his body and blood for them. We speak of this liturgy as commemorating the "institution" of the Lord's supper that has gathered us here so many times before.

But there is another reason why this night is different from all other nights. "Eucharist" is a Greek word that means "thanksgiving." According to one commentator:

> Whatever else this sacrament is, it is a way to give profound thanks to God. On all other occasions we give thanks through the Eucharist for a variety of thing—for the joy of a marriage or for the faithfulness of the life of someone who has died; for protection in time of distress or for success in some important endeavor; for God's mighty acts in Jesus Christ, or for the evidence of divine care in our ordinary days. On all other occasions we give thanks through the Eucharist for many things. But on this night we give thanks *through* the Eucharist *for* the Eucharist itself. Tonight we rejoice above all for this meal which has sustained the faithful for almost 2,000 years.[9]

We rejoice, simply and wonderfully, in the gift of the bread and wine that have become for us the presence of our crucified and risen Lord, the constant reminder of Jesus' presence among his people, for he is truly God-with-us, Emmanuel. We rejoice that the Lord is present with us even in the worst of times, "precisely in those circumstances where we are most likely to forget, or even doubt his abiding love. Tonight we celebrate the Eucharist amid the impending events of the betrayal and denial of our Lord; the next twenty-four hours will see our commemoration of his trial, execution and burial."[10]

How can we rejoice in the midst of that? We cannot rejoice in the events as such, but we do rejoice over their outcome: The Lord triumphs over death and calls us to share in his victory. Every time we celebrate this holy meal we retell, we relive the whole story of tragedy turned to triumph, defeat turned to victory, death turned to life. One commentator put it this way:

> If we can give thanks in the presence of Judas Iscariot who betrays, Simon Peter who denies, and the others who desert, can we not give thanks in all circumstances? The Eucharist sustains us, then, not only in times of obvious joy, but when our hearts are weighed down with any sorrow, temptation, perplexity, failure or fear. For always it is the feast of God's faithfulness and final triumph over evil. It is a foretaste of God's kingdom in the midst of the kingdom of sin and death. How wonderful is this meal—so different from all others. At this table, saints across the ages have been sustained, and sinners reclaimed, so that sinners and saints may share in the Lord's ministry of service to the world.[11]

We must understand that if we dare to eat of the body and drink of the blood of the Lord in the Eucharist, we are called to become his body and blood, at the risk of betrayal and denial and desertion, at the risk of being broken and poured out for the sake of the world, as he was. If we dare to eat of the body and drink of the blood of the Lord, we are called to continue his presence in the world, to be the living signs of his death and resurrection.

Is there any other night like tonight? Is there any other meal like this meal? Is there any better way to give thanks for this ineffable gift than by taking part in it? We give thanks *for* the Eucharist *through* the Eucharist. Blessed be the Lord for this great gift of bread and wine.

## In the Shadow of the Cross

Time: April 16, 1976
Season: Good Friday
Scripture Readings: Isaiah 52:13–53:12;
    Hebrews 4:14–16, 5:7–9; John 18:1–19:42

We stand today in the shadow of the cross.[12] Are you uncomfortable in the presence of the cross? There may be many reasons for feeling uncomfortable: personal sin, psychological reaction to sin and suffering, childhood memories of sermons and catechism lessons, and so forth. Our age has been uncomfortable with the symbol of the cross. We have shied away from the negative aspects of life. We want to affirm the life forces in all their dimensions. We stand for self-affirmation rather than self-denial, for this world rather than for the world to come.

Liberal theology has always recoiled from proclaiming the cross. H. Richard Niebuhr once spoke of the God of liberalism as "a God without wrath who brought men without sin into a kingdom without judgment through the ministrations of a Christ without a cross."[13] This decade seems to have brought a change of mood: a new awareness of the dark and shadowy side of life, of human limitations and human sin, of the continued reality of pain and death, of the mystery of life and of God, a new openness to the symbol of the cross.

The history of Christian theology and piety shows how easily the symbol of the cross can be perverted. Through it the Christian can be led to embrace a concept of God that is theologically idolatrous and psychologically destructive. The symbol of the cross is ambivalent and ambiguous. There is danger in a religious teaching that describes suffering, pain, and death as a just God's punishment for sins, because it is plain that the innocent also suffer. This was recognized as early as the book of Job. Job's friends believe that suffering and misfortune are the result of sin, whereas the whole thrust of Job's dialogues with his companions is that he is not guilty but righteous. If God is responsible for the sufferings of the innocent,

God is made into a demon, and to worship such a God is to worship an executioner. The Christian God has often been pictured this way: one who, to satisfy his justice, decreed that his Son should suffer in our place.

If the suffering of Jesus is seen as God's plan and deliberate choice, a choice freely accepted by Jesus, then suffering can easily be valued for its own sake. Christianity becomes a religion which glorifies suffering, a kind of masochistic cult. The Christian then desires nothing more than to suffer with Christ's suffering, a suffering often conceived in an individual, private, purely internal way. This can be psychologically destructive.

How can we look upon the crucified Jesus, then, in a way that does not distort God beyond recognition and destroy man as we understand God and man today? What is the meaning of the cross for Jesus himself? In the context of Jesus' preaching and ministry, the cross is not something that God directly willed or that Jesus deliberately sought. It is something that happened to Jesus because of human sinfulness and because of his fidelity to his mission. He preached a message of salvation that challenged, disturbed, angered the religious leaders. They reacted by causing his downfall and plotting his death. But the death of Jesus must also be understood politically: Pilate finally interpreted the presence of Jesus as a threat to the state and to his own political future, and so he had him executed.

Did Jesus die because of sin? Yes, if destroying another in fear, protecting one's position at all costs, deciding to sacrifice a human life to preserve the status quo, condemning the innocent to protect one's guilty abuse and possession of power are sinful. Did Jesus die because of my sins? Yes, to the extent that I share in the same attitudes and participate in the same kind of action and decision that today—not nineteen centuries ago—cause pain, rejection, physical harm, mental anguish, physical death, and personal destruction or diminishment of another human being, to a lesser or perhaps even greater extent than when it was done to the man Jesus.

But there is another dimension of the meaning of the cross for Jesus himself: His death constitutes the crisis of everything he stood for. Jesus not only died a political death, rejected by his own people; he died in the unbroken silence of God. The God whom he called Father did not come to save him. He endured with us the death of sin, death experienced as abandonment and separation from God. The evangelist puts on Jesus' lips the words of the psalmist: "My God, my God, why have you forsaken me?"

Who is this God who remained silent as his own Son hung upon a cross to die? Can we accept this kind of God, a God who is free to remain silent even in the midst of our sufferings? Jesus experienced the darkness of feeling abandoned and rejected even by God, the darkest night of the soul. His cross is a symbol that he has become one with us in this. His resurrection is a promise that we will not undergo this darkness alone, that there is light beyond the darkness, but it is not a promise that God will remove the darkness.

In our own time we are profoundly aware of this darkness in the atrocities in Auschwitz, Hiroshima, Vietnam, Lebanon, Northern Ireland. When man's capacity to brutalize his fellow human beings assumes such proportions, the question of God becomes all the more acute. Camus's decision for a godless world where men and women struggle against a universe in which innocent children suffer and die constitutes a challenge that cannot be ignored. For it is not easy to answer a Camus, or a Rubenstein who believes that the God of history was consumed in the flames of the death camps.

Is there an answer? No clear-cut, black-and-white answer, but some reflections. Jesus remained believing and faithful to the silent God who is his Father, even in utter loneliness and crushing death. I think that we can continue to believe in God even after the holocausts of six million people in the gas chambers, precisely because even in the death camps the Shema of Israel, the great daily act of faith of the devout Jew, which begins "Hear, O Israel, Yahweh our God is the one Lord," was still being prayed. And so was the Our Father prayed by Christians facing the same death.

There is an even deeper mystery: If we confess Jesus to be the Son of God, we have to explore the meaning of God's presence on the cross of Jesus, God's personal involvement in that experience of suffering. The cross becomes the final answer to Job's dilemma: God does not instigate our suffering, nor did he decree the suffering of Jesus. Rather he participated in Jesus' suffering. The cross points to a God who is involved in the suffering of his world. Our God is not our executioner but our fellow sufferer.

We do not preach the cross in order to exalt the value of suffering. We do not preach a sadistic God who desired to give up his own Son to death, even for our sake. The suffering of Jesus is not the result of a divine decision but of a human decision. We preach the cross because it is this Jesus and no other who was raised, and it is Christ crucified who has become the power and the wisdom of God.

And we identify with the passion of Jesus not by trying to become emotionally involved in the sufferings of Jesus a long time ago, but rather by trying to locate the passion story as it continues in our world. For our history today is still largely the suffering history of God. To proclaim the cross of Jesus today becomes a summons to accept our responsibility for the present. As the passion story goes on, we are called to participate in it, not as those who cause it, but as those who struggle to free men and women from the oppressions that enslave them.

# Our Part in the Story

TIME: APRIL 18, 1987
SEASON: EASTER VIGIL
SCRIPTURE READINGS: GENESIS 1:1–2:2, 22:1–18;
 EXODUS 14:15–15:1; ISAIAH 54:5–14, 55:1–11;
 BARUCH 3:9–15, 32–4:4; EZEKIEL 36:16–17A, 18–28;
 ROMANS 6:3–11; MATTHEW 28:1–10

On this most holy night, when we remember with longing that night long ago that holds the secret of Jesus being set free from the tomb and entering the glory of God in the fullness of his humanity, we are invited to enter the broad sweep of the history of salvation, retold for us by the Scripture readings.

It begins with the story of creation, which shows God at work, building a universe by word—"let there be"—and by action—"let us make"—naming the works of his creative power and blessing them. The final work is the human creature, made in God's image, male and female. And all of it was good. Then follows the story of human sin and failure, culminating in the flood, and the story of the first covenant between God and the remnant of humanity, the first explicit agreement and promise and personal commitment of God to a continuing creation. This leads to the stories of our ancestors in the faith, summed up in Abraham, the first to believe, the first to hear the promise of a continuing human history in relationship with God, the first to accept this covenant, obedient to the point of being willing to sacrifice his only son, Isaac, as God would one day be willing to suffer the death of his beloved Son on the cross.

The central event of Israel's history is the exodus from Egypt, which our brothers and sisters of Jewish faith have been celebrating this week in the feast of Passover. A helpless group of people, whose only strength is God, faces the might of the Egyptian empire and is set free from slavery by God's mighty hand and outstretched arm. In the desert, on the mountain, with Moses, the covenant, the growing relationship between God and his people is made more explicit, more binding, embracing the whole of life. The law is born, and human beings are given an integral part to play in how history will unfold.

The story continues with times of glory and times of struggle for survival, of fervent faith and gross infidelity, of turning to other gods and returning to God. Eventually the kingdom of Israel is conquered and its tribes dispersed, Jerusalem and the temple are destroyed and its people taken to Babylon in exile. But the prophets who had warned of the impending doom now announce the promise of a new creation, a new exodus, a new covenant. The people will again be led and fed and sustained by God as they once were in the desert. The promise to David will be confirmed, that one of his descendants will always be king over God's people. The marriage bond of the covenant will be renewed, and God's creative word will accomplish all this.

We are here to celebrate that the prophetic word has been fulfilled in a surprising, totally unexpected way: The Word of God has become flesh and dwelt among us; he has died on the cross and been raised from the dead. He leads us by his word and the power of his life; he feeds us with his body and blood; he is enthroned as King of all in the glory of the Father; he is the new creation and the new covenant by which we are called to share his own divine life.

And now we are inserted into the story, called to share in this new creation and new exodus to freedom and new return, not just from exile, but from the realm of death itself. The way we are taken up into this process of salvation is through baptism into Christ's death. How did we get here? What is our own particular story of salvation and relationship with God?

The story of our own journey of sin and rebellion, and of our pilgrimage to faith, is as critical to us individually as the history of salvation is for the world and for the whole human family. By "our story," I mean both our own individual, personal history, and the history of our particular communities of faith, our family, the particular Christian family to which we belong. This question is particularly fitting for the catechumens who will soon confirm publicly their decision for life in the Risen Christ in this particular Christian community, by being baptized or received into the Roman Catholic Christian family.

But our personal story of faith is critical for each of us, for we are all invited to renew our baptismal promises and commitment to the Christian life. One of the benefits of the cycle of yearly festivals in the Church is that we are reminded, and invited, and given the opportunity, again and again, to examine our life and to review our direction and to renew our discipleship of Christ.

I want to invite all of us to reflect on our story of faith. What has brought us here, to this place and this moment of time? By what straight or crooked ways have we traveled? By what secret and hidden and dark passages have we emerged into the light? Who has been our companion and friend? Who has been our guide and witness during our journey? When have we wandered aimlessly? Where have we found ourselves lost? How has God acted in our life; how has he revealed his love to us? How have we changed through the years in our understanding and images and relationships and love of God? What was the last word, the last gesture, the last look that became the invitation that brought us here tonight? What is happening in our mind, in our spirit, in our heart, in our feelings right now?

All that has happened in our life should be focused on this moment of grace, so that we may present to the Lord all that we are and let him take it up into the power of his new life, and hold us in the promise of his new creation, that we may become more truly an Easter people, a people alive in the hope and the joy of the Resurrection.

## The Christ of Faith

Time: April 7, 1996
Season: Easter Sunday
Scripture Readings: Acts 10:34a, 37–43;
    Colossians 3:1–4; John 20:1–9

Do you believe in the Resurrection? Do you believe that the Jesus who died on the cross experienced death as a transforming passage into the glory of a new life? Do you believe that the disciples met Jesus alive and glorious, in an encounter they did not fully understand and could never adequately express and communicate? Do you believe that the resurrection of Jesus is a pledge and a promise that we are called to share Jesus' victory over sin and death, and his new risen life?

This is the Good News that the Church has been announcing for all these centuries, even to this very day. This is the mystery we have gathered to celebrate this morning. As Paul wrote to the Colossians, we have a new life in Christ, although it is hidden in God. But when Christ our life appears, then we shall also appear with him in glory.

Today, faith in the Resurrection is being seriously challenged from within the Christian tradition. There has been an explosion of books and articles focusing on the historical Jesus and challenging the reality of the Resurrection. This past week, three of the major news magazines ran in-depth stories about what has been described as the new search for the historical Jesus.

I have read only the article in *Newsweek*,[14] and I thought it was very well done. It is an excellent survey of what has been published and an intelligent analysis of the implications and significance of this material. The title of the *Newsweek* article, "Rethinking the Resurrection: A New Debate about the Risen Christ," suggests that the Resurrection is at the heart of the current discussion about biblical research.

In their relentless search for the historical Jesus, a number of biblical scholars reject the Gospel stories of the empty tomb

and the resurrection appearances as figments of the imagination of the disciples, developed long after the death of Jesus as evidence of his divinity. The article makes an interesting statement about these scholars and their work that I would like to quote:

> Theirs is not disinterested historical investigation but scholarship with a frankly missionary purpose: by reconstructing the life of Jesus they hope to show that belief in the bodily resurrection of Jesus is a burden to the Christian faith and deflects attention from his role as social reformer.[15]

That is the flaw and the weakness of much of this new and highly publicized biblical research. If we accept its premises, we are left only with the earthly Jesus, because the Christ of faith, the Christ who is the living presence of the eternal God in our human history, is rejected from the start. Without the Resurrection there is no Christ of faith, no Christ, period. There is only the Jesus of history, the earthly Jesus.

What do we have when we discover the Jesus of history? According to one author, we have a "peasant philosopher preaching an inclusive kingdom of God among Israel's outcasts."[16] There have been many peasant philosophers in the course of history who are now barely remembered. According to another author, Jesus was actually the "wicked priest" mentioned in the Qumran scrolls. This reconstruction of a fertile imagination has no reality, no attraction, no future. The Qumran scrolls are all that remains of a religious sect that disappeared during the first century, while Christianity continues to flourish and to give meaning to the lives of billions of people. For another author, Jesus was a charismatic figure, a healer, sage, and prophet, who founded a movement to revitalize religion.[17] All these contemporary interpretations of the historical Jesus fail to explain the rise, the development, and the present vitality of the Christian faith.

Is the Risen Christ a reality or only the creation of Peter's overwhelming grief and guilt, of a series of interpsychic experiences on the part of the disciples? That is the question, and it cannot be answered on the basis of critical biblical research, psychological reconstructions, or sociological analysis. The only answer to the question of the reality of the Risen Christ is the answer of faith.

I do believe in the resurrection of Jesus. I do believe the Risen Christ is a reality. I do not attempt to argue that the Resurrection can be established scientifically or by using historical criteria. But I would argue that scientific and historical knowledge is not the only kind of knowledge available to us as human beings. I would argue, theologically, that without the Resurrection there would be no Christ of faith. And I would argue, historically, that without the Christ of faith there would have been no Christian movement in the first century and no Christianity today.

I do not bring up this issue of the problems raised by some of the research into the historical Jesus out of academic interest or intellectual curiosity. The question of faith in the Risen Christ has a tremendous, immediate impact on our daily life, on how we define ourselves and discover meaning in our life. The question I ask myself is this: Where would I be, what kind of person would I be, what would happen to my life if there were no Risen Christ, if Jesus were nothing more than another historical figure whose life is recorded in history as a series of past events? What would happen to my life if there were no Risen Christ present here and now, in this gathering, in this community, and in my heart?

I know that there are many women and men who find meaning and purpose, direction and satisfaction, ideals of generosity and compassion, and who are able to construct a very worthwhile life, without faith in Jesus as the Risen Christ, as the one who comes to reveal to the world the saving love of God. I am just asking for myself, and I invite you to ask for yourself: What would life be without the Risen Christ?

Think of the Gospel that was proclaimed this morning. What would have happened to Mary Magdalene if she had been convinced that the body of Jesus had been stolen from the tomb, if she had never had the experience of Jesus calling her by name once again and revealing himself to her as living in a new and glorious life? What would have happened to Peter and the other disciple if they had come running to the tomb, found it empty, decided that the body of the dead Jesus had been stolen, and had gone about trying to find it? I can only imagine emptiness and defeat, grief and despair, a terrible sense of loss and disappointment, that slowly, painfully, gradually recedes to the background as they go back to their previous, ordinary life.

If there were no Risen Christ, no Christ of faith, the very center of my life would be missing. I would feel a terrible sense of emptiness where his presence is now, a deep sense of longing for a friend who has never failed to be by my side, for a teacher whose words go deep into my heart to inspire me and challenge me, for a guide who leads me into new discoveries and adventures. I suspect that I would find other realities to give meaning and purpose to my existence, such as my gifts and responsibilities as a human being, my solidarity with the human family, ideals of mutual respect and love for my brothers and sisters.

But now in the earthly Jesus I have the one human being who has embodied for me the very ideal of being human, who lived his life for the sake of others, who was not afraid to face death for the sake of his sisters and brothers. And in the Risen Christ, the Christ of faith, this Jesus has revealed himself to be more than human, to be the one in whom "the fullness of God was pleased to dwell bodily," and has told us that he continues to be with us, to work with us, to empower us by sharing with us his own victory over evil and death, by sharing with us the power of his new life.

How about you? What is the meaning of the Risen Christ in your life? What would life feel like without the presence of Christ? I invite you to reflect on this question for yourself. But even more, I invite you to rejoice and be glad because in fact Jesus was raised from the dead by the power of God, and the Risen Christ is present here in our midst, and he continues to reveal to us in his person the tender love and the infinite saving power of our God.

In faith we proclaim: Christ is risen, Alleluia! He is risen indeed, Alleluia!

# The Requirements of Community

Time: April 26, 1987
Season: Second Sunday of Easter
Scripture Readings: Acts 2:42–47; 1 Peter 1:3–9; John 20:19–31

We give joyful praise and thanks to God for the catechumens who were baptized and received into the Church during the Easter Vigil liturgy. They were added to our number and became part of this community of salvation. We rejoice in their presence among us, and that presence continues to be a reminder for all of us of our rebirth to hope, the gift of new life that comes through the resurrection of Jesus Christ that we received in baptism. We give thanks and praise to God for having called us to know and to share the life of his beloved Son, Jesus Christ.

Using the texts of today's liturgy, I would like to make two points about this new life which we have received in baptism, about the salvation to which we have been called. The first point is that salvation and life in Christ is a continuing process, not a once-and-for-all, final state. The American psychologist William James wrote: "Truth *happens* to be an idea. It *becomes* true, is *made* true by events. Its verity is in fact an event, a process."

The First Letter of Peter could be described as being about a "truth" that "became true," a process by which an idea becomes a reality. Many scholars are of the opinion that the first part of the letter is taken from an early baptismal liturgy, and most of the letter examines what it means in practice to be baptized, how our life should be different because of our baptism. In today's reading, the first paragraph is a hymn of praise, but the second paragraph reminds us that the gift of faith will be tested by many trials, as gold is tested by fire. Faith is a precious gift, but it is only a beginning, like the planting of a seed that must grow to the fullness of life with the Risen Christ. Only then will our salvation be completed.

As long as we live in this world we have to continue the process begun by the gift of God until it reaches its fullness. What is begun in baptism must be carried through to the end, when God will complete the work he has begun in us. In the meantime we must continue to live out the reality of our baptism in our everyday life, by believing in Jesus, and loving him, and obeying him; by being in touch with his constant presence in our life, attentive and responsive to his invitations and suggestions. The gift of faith and new life in baptism needs to grow in us every day of our life.

The second point is the indispensable function of the Christian community. The first reading is one of three summaries found in the book of Acts that describe the Church in its infancy. (The Gospel of Luke and the book of the Acts of the Apostles are like two volumes of the same work. In the Gospel we have the story of the work of the Spirit of God in the life and ministry of Jesus. In the Acts we have the story of the Spirit at work in the early Church.) It is the same Spirit at work in Jesus and in the community of those who believe in him. The Good News is an unfolding, developing story, and it is God who is at work in his Church, as he was in Jesus.

Today's reading gives us four crucial elements in the life of the Church, mentioned in the opening verse and enlarged in the verses that follow. They are: (1) the apostles' instructions, (2) the communal life, (3) the breaking of bread, and (4) the prayers. The apostles' preaching is one of the wonders that attracts people to this small band of believers and adds to their number. It is the way that Jesus is made present, his story told, his work of salvation proclaimed. The communal life is evident in the sharing of all things. When there is a need, those who have more sell some of their property and the community is able to provide for those in need. The breaking of the bread is a reference to the celebration of the Eucharist: It takes place in their homes, after they have prayed and given witness in the temple area. They pray together with exultant and sincere hearts, giving praise to God.

This is an idealized portrait of the early Christian community, also described in another summary as being of one heart and mind, selfless in the love they share. We know from the material that will follow that this was not always the reality. But the ideal remains, even for us. We are called to be that kind of a community. Even though we fall short of the ideal, we must continue to strive for it; and we ask the Lord for forgiveness for our failures and for the grace to grow toward the kind of community he wants us to be.

The preaching and the teaching of the bishops and the pope, who now function for us as the college of the apostles functioned for the early Church, is still the best assurance that the Good News of Jesus Christ is proclaimed properly and faithfully; it is still the instrument and the sign of unity in the community of faith. The way we care for one another and for those who are in need must become an ever clearer sign and witness to the love of the Lord operating in our midst. Our breaking of bread together, our celebrations of the Eucharist, should be the crowning moment of our communal life, the most powerful way to become one in mind and heart in the sharing of the body and blood of the Lord. And whenever we come together, for any reason, prayer should always be part of our gathering, as an expression of our joy and praise to God who has called us to be his community, his holy people.

May the Risen Lord, who is in our midst, in whom we believe, whom we love, even though we do not see him, dispel all fear and fill our minds and our hearts with his peace. And may we become more and more the channels and the instruments of his compassion and reconciliation and new life.

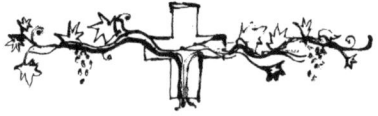

# Walking with the Risen Lord

Time: April 9, 1978
Season: Third Sunday of Easter
Scripture Readings: Acts 2:14, 22–33; 1 Peter 1:17–21;
Luke 24:13–35

Father Nolan, commenting on today's Gospel reading, stated: "Some gospels like this one are so rich we could preach a dozen sermons (and unfortunately some preachers try)." It is truly a little masterpiece, the most beautiful of the appearance stories. I will try to focus on the liturgical implications of this story, which is found only in Luke. The story developed from an original nucleus of disciples experiencing the presence of the Risen Jesus, through various stages of the growth of faith and understanding of the mystery of the continuing presence of the living Lord with his community. Finally, Luke, with artistic literary skill, made it into a vivid narrative.

In its present form, the story reflects the pattern of early Christian worship. Look at these elements: The disciples' attention is centered on the meaning of the life of Jesus and the tragedy of his death; the Scriptures, the biblical word of God, are proclaimed and explained so that a new insight can grow; the disciples gather around a table and bread is broken with a sacred gesture and the word of blessing. In Luke and Acts, "the breaking of the bread" is a term used for the Eucharist. This does not mean that Jesus celebrated the Eucharist with the two disciples at Emmaus. Rather, the narrative has been constructed and adapted to reflect the early liturgy.

Why? Why would the author do this? Why would Luke deliberately describe a resurrection appearance as if it had happened in a liturgical setting, with the structure of a eucharistic liturgy, as celebrated in the early church, and as we celebrate it today? For a very good reason: because the disciples believed that the Risen Lord was present with the community of his disciples in the celebration of the Eucharist; because they believed that Jesus, alive again after his death on the cross, was met not only in the extraordinary appearances to the two Marys, and to Peter, and to the Twelve in the supper room, and to Thomas who doubted, but also by the whole community every time it gathered for the memorial celebration of the Lord's Supper, of the breaking of the bread. The story is designed to tell us that every time we gather to celebrate the great act of praise and thanksgiving which we call the Eucharist, we meet the Risen Lord, as the two disciples did.

Is that not an incredibly beautiful insight for us? Here we are, we are doing what the two disciples did with the risen Jesus, and the same Risen Lord is doing the same thing with us today. For the first readers of Luke's Gospel this story would have been immediately evident. For us it may need a little explanation. How did the early Christians believe that Jesus was present with his believers gathered for the Eucharist? In three ways.

Jesus had said to his disciples: Where two or three of you are gathered in my name, there I am in the midst of you. The two persons walking along the road to Emmaus in today's Gospel are disciples who had followed Jesus, and now they are talking about him, their attention is focused on him, the moment is centered on Jesus: They are reliving the great climax of his life. And Jesus joins them. There is a kind of presence that is brought into being by the community coming together in the name of Jesus, to remember him, a remembrance that brings the past into the present and allows us to experience again, to relive now a moment, an event, of his life. It is a mysterious presence, not always easy to recognize and to feel and to acknowledge. But it grows more explicit through what happens as we go along.

The second way in which the Risen Lord is present with his worshipping community is through the proclamation, the explanation, and the hearing of the Word of God. In the Gospel story, Jesus enters into the conversation of the two disciples, and he interprets the Bible, Moses and the prophets, so that they will understand better who he is and what had happened. And the two will say later: "Were not our hearts burning inside us as he talked to us on the road and explained

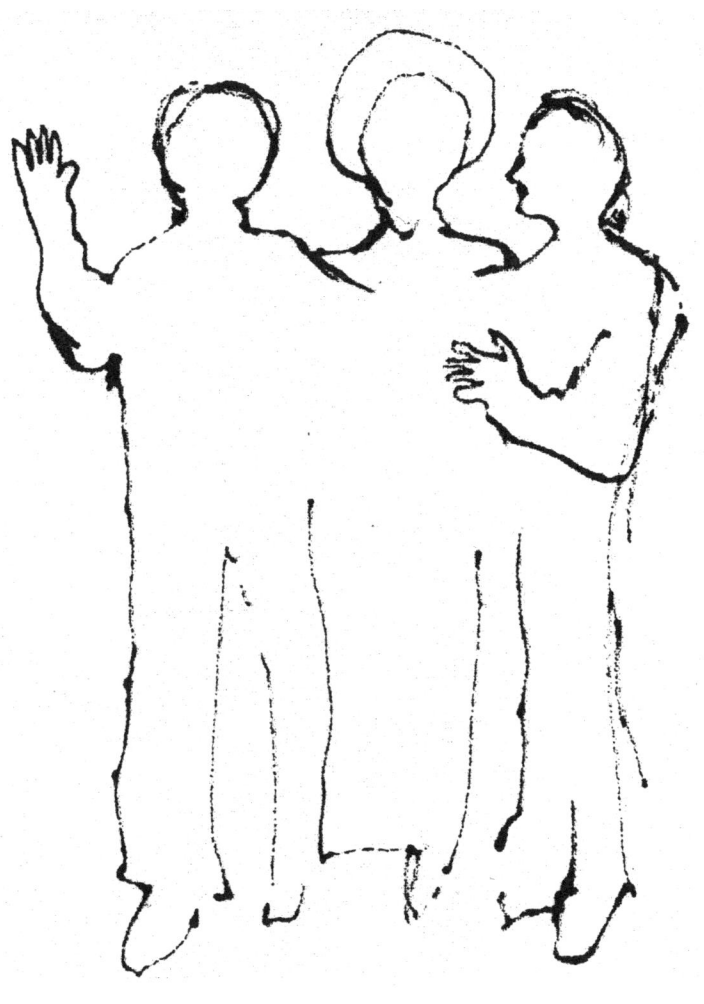

the Scriptures to us?" (v. 32). Jesus becomes present to the heart and mind of the believer through the hearing and the understanding of the sacred Word of the Bible, of the Scriptures, as they are proclaimed and explained.

The third way in which Jesus, who died and was raised from the dead, is present with those who are gathered in his name is through the sacramental signs, the breaking of the bread of Eucharist and communion. The disciples have become aware of an extraordinary presence in the stranger who has shared their journey and interpreted the meaning of Jesus through the explanation of the Scriptures. They want to remain in that presence; they ask him to stay. And seated at the table they finally come to full recognition in the breaking of the bread. The gestures, the language, the action, the mystery are the same as found in the traditions of the Last Supper and in the celebration of the Eucharist ever since.

By baptism we are constituted and established as the community that experiences and proclaims the presence of the Risen Lord. By baptism we are called and designated to be disciples of Jesus, just as the two whose ancient story we have heard this morning. It is possible to believe in Jesus without being baptized, but the official seal and expression of that faith in Jesus is baptism. The Church is the community of the baptized. People may want to either broaden or narrow the meaning of the Church, but it is that. By baptism we are called to belong formally and explicitly to this community that continues to encounter the Risen Lord in worship.

By baptism we are introduced to, or given, or enter into a new relationship with the Word of God. Because we are baptized, the story of Jesus becomes our story; his history is our history. We are no longer interested observers, objective outsiders studying ancient traditions out of historical, or cultural, or sociological, or literary interest. It is not like listening to the story of events that have not touched us in any way. Because by baptism we have, in some mysterious but real way, been incorporated, made part of Jesus, the Risen Christ. His life is our life; his death is our deliverance; his resurrection is our hope. The Word of God is the story of our origins and of our destiny, of our being and of our becoming, of our roots and of our bearing fruit.

Has the Word of God ever made your heart burn within you? Has it ever had such impact on you that you felt like a new person, strengthened to live differently? Sometimes, at least, the Word comes with clarity and power, surprising in its relevance to human life, dramatically alive, experienced as new life. The Word of God is the presence of the Risen Jesus here and now.

By baptism we are invited to table fellowship with the Lord, to share the bread broken, the cup blessed. We are on a journey, and the Lord is with us. We have celebrated his presence by gathering in his name and listening to his word. We now ask him to remain with us so that we may recognize him in the breaking of the bread.

## The Lord Is My Shepherd

TIME: APRIL 20, 1975
SEASON: FOURTH SUNDAY OF EASTER
SCRIPTURE READINGS: ACTS 2:14A, 36–41;
1 PETER 2:20B–25; JOHN 10:1–10

The Scripture readings for today's Mass come to us from the last quarter of the first century. These three readings give us an indication of the variety of ways in which the Christian communities at that time understood the meaning of Jesus in relationship to themselves.

The first reading, from the book of Acts, gives us the conclusion of the first proclamation of Peter on the day of Pentecost. We are told that his hearers were deeply shaken by Peter's statement that God has made Jesus both Lord and Messiah. We would be shaken, too, if all of a sudden we were made to realize that this man who was nailed to the cross as a criminal now is presented as Lord and Messiah. It is no wonder that they asked: "What are we to do?"

This image of Jesus as Lord has been preserved in Christian tradition. In the imagery of the Eastern church, especially in the great mosaics of the Byzantine period, we find Jesus portrayed as the Pantokrator or Lord and ruler of all, as a king robed in splendor with the keys of power and the scepter of justice. There is a magnificent mosaic in the cathedral of Cefalu in Sicily that dates from the 11$^{th}$ or 12$^{th}$ century with an inscription that describes this perspective very well. Jesus, the Lord of all, says: "I, the maker and the redeemer of what I have made, having myself a body, judge the body and the souls of men, for I am God." The Shrine of the Immaculate Conception in Washington, D.C., which is regarded as the national Roman Catholic cathedral, also has a great image of Jesus as Lord and ruler of all.

The second reading, in a very severe contrast, presents a totally different image of Jesus: Jesus as the suffering servant, quoting from the fourth song of Isaiah on the suffering servant (chap. 53), describing how we are healed by his bruises and saved by his death. Here, Peter is talking to Christians who are suffering great distress and severe persecution, and he is using the memory of the suffering of Jesus, the saving power of his death, as strength and comfort for the Christian community in its time of suffering.

The favorite image of Jesus for the early Christians in Rome was the good shepherd. The catacombs, the underground burial places where the Christians gathered to both hide and worship, and where they lined up their dead, many of whom had died in persecution, have on their walls line drawings of the good shepherd. You will also find the image painted in some areas. And, if I remember correctly, the first statue of Jesus that has come down to us from those times is the statue of the good shepherd, a young man with the sheep on his shoulders and with joy on his face at having found the sheep that was lost.

The image of the good shepherd is found in the Old Testament as well. The well-known psalm that we recited this morning speaks of the Lord as the shepherd of Israel. Ezekiel in his prophecy announces that the Lord himself will gather all the lost and the strays on a dark, cloudy day and bring them back to their land. It's a beautiful and moving image.

We may have problems with the image of the shepherd and the sheep. For one thing, it is not a very familiar image to us. I doubt that many of us have had experience herding sheep. And words are tricky things. A slight variation can destroy the power of the image. There is a story told about Bishop Gorman, who was born and raised in the great metropolis of Los Angeles, and who probably had never seen a sheep in his life. He was appointed Bishop of Reno, and one day he was in a church for confirmation with a community which was mostly Basque. And so, he thought, here was his great chance to really preach and elaborate this magnificent idea of Jesus as the good shepherd. As he was going on at great length, he realized that the children were staring at him blankly. So, he turned to them and said, "Surely, you know what a shepherd is." After a few moments, one said, "Oh, you mean a sheep herder."

The image also may have for us connotations of dull and blind following that we may find difficult to reconcile with our understanding and feeling about the dignity of human persons. But there are elements in this image that I think are very appropriate for our own time and our own experience. Psalm 23 says: "Even though I walk in the dark valley, I fear no evil, for you are at my side." So this imagery also involves the sense of a companion, a loving and faithful companion, who walks our road with us. And the Gospel of John makes a contrast between the thief who comes in to steal and to destroy and his own relationship to the flock: His coming is for life. Jesus came to give life so that we might have life and have it more abundantly. It is the possibility of fullness of human life, the fullness of life with God, that is the gift of the shepherd.

And then we have that beautiful phrase: "The sheep hear his voice as he calls his own by name." The sheep follow him because they recognize his voice. This is literally true, but I think for us it can convey a sense of intimate and personal and loving knowledge. This is what the usage of names in the Old Testament says to us. Yahweh, for instance, always knows his chosen ones by name, and when the occasion arises, when a new task is given to a person, or when God enters into a new relationship with a person, Yahweh often changes the name of the person to reflect the change in relationship. For many people, to know the name of a person is related to knowing who the person is. To know a person's name gives a sense of power over that person, simply because one can name the person, identify the person by name both in blessings and in curses. But if that is true, then to reveal one's name, to let another person know one's name, is also a sign of trust and confidence.

The Gospel tells us through the imagery that Jesus the good shepherd calls his own by name, that he knows us personally and intimately and lovingly, even as we sit here this morning. For we are not simply an unnamed crowd. We are not simply a number stenciled on a shirt or a set of holes punched in a computer card. For Jesus, we are named, each one an individual, a particular person who hears himself or herself called and who answers. I wish I could call each of you by name. I can't. That's my limitation, but that's not the Lord's limitation. He knows each of you by name. I'm sure we understand how important this is when we think of our own human relationships, how difficult it is to respond pleasantly and lovingly to someone who calls us, "Hey, you." To remember that in the master and slave relationship, the standard address to the slave was "Boy," precisely to indicate that he was not quite human. Certainly not quite the person the master was.

How important it is to us when another makes an effort to remember our name, when another makes an effort to know what we want to be called, how we want to be addressed. It is a sign that they are taking an interest in us, that they are seeing us as an individual with all the ties and the background, the good and the bad, the sadness and the joy that go into making us what we are.

This is what Jesus is—not only to the Christians of the first century, but to us. He is Lord and shepherd. He is guardian of our souls. He is the suffering servant. He is the one who has power and dominion over us, but he has that power and dominion because he has given his life for us, because he has gone through the dark valley with us, because he loves us and knows us personally, because he is not a stranger but a friend.

So, with the Christians of the first century, we can express our faith by saying: "Jesus is Lord," but we also know in faith and love that the Lord is our shepherd. May God bless us.

## Empowered by the Resurrection

Time: May 5, 1996
Season: Fifth Sunday of Easter
Scripture Readings: Acts 6:1–7; 1 Peter 2:4–9;
John 14:1–12

The great fifty days of Easter are a continuing celebration of the complex, mysterious event of the resurrection of Jesus, of his appearances to the disciples, of his return to the Father and exaltation at God's right hand, and of the gift of the Holy Spirit. It is one great event, and in some of the Gospel narratives, as in the Gospel of John, it is presented as a single happening. In another sense, it is an event that is extended throughout the rest of history, if we see it as the passage from the ministry of Jesus to the ministry of the Church, a ministry that continues today, in us and through us. The Father who lives in Jesus and has accomplished his works through him will now accomplish even greater works through the disciples, through those who believe in Jesus. Reginald Fuller, commenting on this Gospel passage in the context of the liturgy, writes:

> For us, the important message of today's [Gospel passage] is that the risen, exalted Christ continues in his church his words and works. Are these greater works, the word and sacrament, greater because they will actually mediate the divine salvation whereas in the earthly Jesus his words and works only pointed forward to and prepared the central saving acts? His departure from earth was preparatory for his continual coming to his church.[18]

What is wrong with us, as Church, today? Why is the Risen Lord's presence in the world in and through his Church not more evident, more compelling, more easily grasped and acknowledged? Where are the greater works that we who believe in Jesus as our Risen Lord are supposed to be doing? Why are not the word and sacrament more effective, more life-giving, more powerful in transforming the Church and the whole world into the new creation, into the fullness of God's kingdom of salvation for all?

The answer is that we are human, limited, sinful, and we still fall into the temptation that Jesus rejected so emphatically and categorically in his own time: the temptation to use the power of God at work in us for our own advantage and gain, for our own glory and praise, instead of recognizing that whatever power we have is God's power, not our own, a power that can be used only for the praise and glory of God and in the service of God's people, especially those who are weakest and have no power of their own.

The first reading tells us that this human face of the Church appeared in the community of Jesus believers from the very beginning of its existence. Several passages in the book of Acts describe the early Church in very ideal ways: The believers were all of one mind and one heart, united in prayer and in the breaking of the bread, devoted to the teaching of the apostles, sharing all things in common, so that no one was in need (Acts 2:42–47; 4:32–35). At the beginning of chapter 6, we find the first evidence of conflict and division as suggested by our first reading. Differences are becoming more apparent and creating problems. Some people speak Hebrew (or Aramaic), and others speak Greek. Some are very strong in their Jewish identity, and others have become acculturated to the prevailing Greco-Roman way of life.

The Hellenists, those who speak Greek, complain that their widows are not getting a fair share of the food distributed each day. But, as the unfolding of the story makes very clear, the differences are deeper than just a fair share of material goods. There are questions about the importance of the Jerusalem temple and the value of the accepted Jewish traditions, about the meaning and the reach of the mission received from Jesus: Should the believers be content to stay in Jerusalem and continue their familiar life, or should they go forth in every direction to proclaim the Good News of God's saving work in Jesus? The Hellenists want a voice in the life of the early Christian community, a share in the decision-making power.

Is anything like this happening in the Church today? Are differences in language creating divisions in our parishes? Are there groups in the Church that feel disenfranchised and without a voice? Are there conflicts and power struggles in the Body of Christ today? You know as well as I do how divided we are as Christians. We are divided by historical traditions into Catholic and Orthodox and Protestant; we are divided within the same traditions into liberal and conservative, progressive and traditional, fundamentalist and non-fundamentalist. But perhaps we need to bring these questions closer to home and ask: Are there conflicts and divisions in this community of believers in Jesus? Are there different groups in this parish community vying for power, trying to gain advantage in the way ministries and services are distributed, in the way resources are allocated?

Today I am just a visitor in your midst, so it is easier for me to raise the questions, because I do not know what your situation is, and I am in no position to suggest any answers. I must leave that to you, to your honest reflection and open dialogue. There is nothing wrong with the fact that there are differences and tensions, and that there may be conflicts and divisions. The book of Acts today tells us that this was a reality in the first community of disciples of Christ in Jerusalem, when the original apostles were still present among them. An important aspect of a Christian community is to be able to recognize openly and honestly the differences and the power struggles that are bound to arise, and to deal with them openly and in a spirit of mutual acceptance, respect, and love.

How did the apostles deal with the conflict related in today's first reading? They empowered those who felt neglected and powerless. They shared their leadership with the Hellenists, at a deeper level than just taking charge of the food distribution. In the verse that immediately follows today's passage, Stephen, one of the newly appointed leaders, begins to preach, reinterpreting the history of Israel and questioning the place and value of the temple for the worship of God. After Stephen is killed, while the apostles remain in Jerusalem, the newly chosen leaders, driven by persecution, begin to spread out in the surrounding regions to preach the Good News of Jesus.

As Catholics we have just barely begun this process of sharing power and leadership in the Church, and I truly do not know how fast we will move and how far we will go. Much depends on the willingness of the hierarchical structures to share their power, but there is much that can be done at the level of the local community to try to make sure that no one is left out, no one is neglected, no one is made to feel like a minority, without the same dignity as the prevailing group, without the same access to doing God's work, without the same right to God's word and sacrament.

The second reading gives us the magnificent ideal of what we are, as individuals and as a Christian community. This is the very foundation of all that we do, of the very power that enables us to do the greater works that we are called to do for God. The First Letter of Peter tells the newly baptized that they are "a chosen race, a royal priesthood, a consecrated nation, a people he claims for his own to proclaim the glorious works of the One who called [them] from darkness into his marvelous light" (2:9). We are God's royal priesthood and consecrated nation.

We are the new temple being built on the cornerstone that is Christ Jesus. If only we could grasp fully what this means to us as a community and as individuals, the power that comes from our baptism, as well as the mission, the responsibility, the task that is ours, how different the Christian Church would be, how different our parish communities would become! Is it possible? Can we do it? Yes, we can, if we are willing to go back to our roots, to make our own, again and again, the great saving event that we celebrate during this Easter season, to put our whole trust in the Risen Christ who continues to come to us, his Church, who is always here for us, who is our way, our truth, our life.

# If You Love Me

TIME: MAY 24, 1987
SEASON: SIXTH SUNDAY OF EASTER
SCRIPTURE READINGS: ACTS 8:5–8, 14–17; 1 PETER 3:15–18; JOHN 14:15–21

"If you love me," says Jesus in today's Gospel, "you will keep my commandments." In that sentence lies a summary of Christian faith and life. "If you love me . . . ." That's Christian faith in a nutshell: Christians are people who love Jesus. Whatever our race, age, background, way of thinking, traditions, we are people for whom Jesus is normative and determinative. Whatever the differences might be among us, if we call ourselves Christians we must be people who love Jesus, who love his way of being in the world, who accept Jesus' life, teaching and ministry, suffering, death and resurrection as the deciding factor for our lives.

"If you love me . . ." is the condition for our Christian faith, and the second part of the sentence is the expression of our Christian commitment, "you will keep my commandments." Christians are not only people who love Jesus, but also people who keep his word, his commandments. That is the uniqueness of Christian ethics, the challenge of a Christian life lived out in faith. We must try to keep Jesus' word and live as he lived. Loving Jesus is acted out in love, the love that he modeled for us in his own life. Faith and love, commitment and action go together. Faith without ethical commitment and action is shallow, superficial, and insincere. Ethical commitment without faith can be misdirected and lifeless.

Because he loved Jesus and wanted to keep his word, Philip—one of the leaders of the Hellenistic group, whom we saw appointed to special ministry in last Sunday's reading—when he is driven out of Jerusalem by persecution, moves into Samaria and there proclaims the word and does the works of Jesus. And then the Jerusalem Jewish-Christian community reaches out generously and joyfully to the Samaritans, a people from whom they had been separated historically by mutual hostility, distrust, and hatred. That is the love of Jesus in action.

The author of the First Letter of Peter is writing to new Christians who find themselves in a hostile environment and are experiencing misunderstanding and active persecution. In the preceding verses the author speaks with particular power and poignancy when he says that the Christian should not return evil for evil, or insult for insult, but rather should return a blessing, and be loving toward the other, kindly disposed and humble. The two verses preceding today's text read: "Now who will harm you if you are eager to do what is good? But even if you do suffer for doing what is right, you are blessed" (1 Pet. 3:13–14a). This is the kind of life and behavior that will lead people to ask for the reason for our hope.

The directive in today's passage: "Always be ready to give an explanation to anyone who asks you for a reason for your hope, but do it with gentleness and reverence," has become a cliché for a certain type of Christian who feels called and obligated to confront others at every occasion with the question of faith in Jesus Christ. I have heard these words used almost as a battle cry for proselytizing by those who forget that this passage suggests that we should wait for the other to ask us about our faith and our hope and our joy, and that our reply should be filled with gentle respect for the other person. I am more convinced than ever that the only effective witness is the witness of our life, a life lived in keeping the words of Jesus because we truly love him.

In recent years, the publication of the diary of Etty Hillesum, a young Jewish woman who died in Auschwitz in 1943, has been for many people the channel for a profound encounter with God's grace, especially in the midst of tremendous suffering. From the concentration camp at Westerbork, Holland, before being sent east, Etty wrote:

> It has been brought home forcibly to me here how every atom of hatred added to the world makes it an even more inhospitable place. And I also believe, childishly perhaps, but stubbornly, that the earth will become more habitable again only through the love that the Jew Paul described to the citizens of Corinth in the thirteenth chapter of his letter.[19]

This refusal to hate, this determination to love, wherever and whenever it occurs, is the strongest witness to the presence of God, to the hope that is in our hearts.

The sentence I quoted from the second reading is followed by the injunction: "Keep your conscience clear." This is what I want to say when I speak of the witness of our life: There is no way that we can speak convincingly and effectively of Jesus Christ if our words are not supported by the way we live. Is our conscience clear? Does our conscience tell us that we live according to the words and the model of Jesus? Can we say that our conscience is clear, that we live as Jesus wants us to live in our marriage and family relationships, in the way we live our sexuality, in our friendships and love, in our work and profession, in our honesty and truthfulness, in our concern for the poor and the weak and the marginal in our society? Does our conscience tell us that we are serious about living a simple life, one not dominated by greed and possessions and inordinate desires for material things? Is our conscience clear in our commitment to the cause of justice and the building of peace, in our commitment to work to assure the possibility of human life with freedom and dignity and respect for all our sisters and our brothers?

"If you love me, you will keep my commandments." As we prepare to celebrate the Eucharist, we make ready to receive again and welcome into our life the Risen Christ. We come out of love, seeking to have our love deepened. We come out of faith, seeking to have our faith strengthened. We pray not only that we might be prepared to receive Christ in the Eucharist, but also that we might hear his command for each of us and be empowered by him to keep his word, to do his will in our lives.

# The Cosmic Christ

Time: May 31, 1987
Season: Seventh Sunday of Easter
Scripture Readings: Acts 1:12–14; 1 Peter 4:13–16; John 17:1–11a

Every year hundreds of thousands of people rejoice and celebrate as "their" team wins the World Series, the Super Bowl, the Stanley Cup, the NBA championship, the NCAA or NIT tournament. There is an infectious, at times wild, sense of vicarious satisfaction in identifying with the winner: it is a way of sharing in the victory, of basking in the glory of the team or the extraordinary feats of an individual.

This is not the kind of glory for which Jesus prays in today's Gospel reading, the glory he shares with the Father, the glory his disciples are called to share. Jesus is not asking for victory parades and banner headlines, for adulation and acclamation, for praise and rewards for what he has done. For the Israelites the glory of God was the luminous cloud that overshadowed the tabernacle, the Holy of Holies, as a sign of God's presence.

In the Gospel of John, God's glory is still the presence of God, the presence of God's salvation—but now it fills not only the temple but the whole world with new hope, new life, and grace. And God's salvation is Jesus Christ, the eternal Word that was with God and was God, and became flesh in him, who now has been raised from the dead and has returned, as redeemed humanity, to the glory of the Father.

In the readings for the feast of the Ascension this past week, we heard the phrase from the letter of Paul to the Ephesians that described Jesus as the fullness that fills the universe in all its parts. It is for this that Jesus is praying to the Father, for his saving presence to permeate and transform all being and all becoming, all that is and all that is yet to be.

This all-pervasive and transforming presence of Jesus in the world has been called the "Cosmic Christ." Perhaps we are not sufficiently conscious of this cosmic dimension of the mystery of Christ, especially if we focus exclusively on the personal, singular, individual dimension of our relationship with the Lord. The Cosmic Christ is more than the mysterious, undefinable divine presence of the Creator to his creation. The Cosmic Christ is the Risen Jesus, freed by the Resurrection from the limitations of earthly existence, now made available for the whole universe as the power of creative transformation, as the presence of the saving love of God at work everywhere in the universe—changing it from within, making it new, preparing the new creation, the promised new heavens and new earth, where there will be no more tears, no more mourning, no more death.

Teilhard de Chardin speaks of this reality as the "Christogenesis of St. Paul." He attributes it to St. Paul because he uses much of the thought of Paul from the letters to the Romans, Ephesians, and Colossians as the basis for his vision. Teilhard coins the term "Christogenesis" from the word "cosmogenesis" that is part of his evolutionary theory. Cosmogenesis describes the world in the making, the becoming of the universe through the process of evolution. By "Christogenesis" Teilhard wants to say that from a spiritual perspective, from the vision of faith, we should see that the universe is centered in Christ and moving toward a total union in him, being transformed into him.

According to Teilhard, this transformation into Christ does not come about through some distant divine action. On the contrary, it takes place through the immanent presence, the presence within, of the human, personal reality of the Risen Christ. Teilhard compares this presence of Christ in the world to his presence in the Eucharist, where Jesus becomes really, personally present in his risen humanity all over the world. And when Jesus comes sacramentally to each of us, it is not only for a private conversation with the one receiving the sacrament. According to Teilhard,

> It is to join him more to himself, physically, and to all other faithful in the growing unity of the world. When he says through the priest "This is my Body,". . . the priestly action extends beyond the transubstantiated Host to the cosmos

itself, which the still unfinished Incarnation gradually transforms in the course of the passing centuries.[20]

On one occasion during a scientific expedition in the Ordos Desert of China, when he found it impossible to say Mass, Teilhard wrote the beautiful *Mass on the World*, where the universe is "an immense Host" and Christ "an Energy *quae possit sibi omnia subjicere*" [that can bring all things under his power], "an influence secretly present in the depths of matter and a dazzling Centre."[21]

To go one step further: One of the ways in which the human, personal presence of the Risen Christ becomes part of the world is through the Eucharist, as Christ unites himself in Holy Communion with us and with all the faithful throughout the world and throughout history, and in us and through us becomes present in the physical world.

It is easy to be so overwhelmed by the seemingly insurmountable problems in the world that we are tempted to despair and to retreat into our own little world. It is natural to be so preoccupied with our personal problems that we are unable to see this process of transformation and redemption at work in the world. But it is unfortunate if we become so absorbed with our own personal destiny and salvation, or with our own community of faith, or with the institutional Church, that we are not interested in the destiny and salvation of the world.

From time to time we need to be reminded of this cosmic vision: "God so loved the world that he gave his only Son . . . that the world might be saved through him" (John 3:16–17). The *world* is to be saved through Christ—not just me or people like me. In the words of Paul, "all creation groans and is in agony" awaiting the fullness of redemption (Rom. 8:19–23).

We pray that this glorious, saving, transforming presence of the Risen Christ, who is at the right hand of the Father, will grow everywhere and hasten the day of the fullness of redemption. We pray that we will be faithful to this word of promise, to this ultimate hope that has been entrusted to us to share with the world. We pray that the Eucharist we receive today will change us and make us the human, personal, loving presence of the Christ of glory in our world.

# Using Our Gifts

TIME: JUNE 7, 1987
SEASON: PENTECOST
SCRIPTURE READINGS: ACTS 2:1–11;
   1 CORINTHIANS 12:3B–7, 12–13; JOHN 20:19–23

The Church, in its liturgical practice, puts the Feast of Pentecost on a par with Easter as one of the two most important days of the year for our spiritual life. But the cultural experience of the two holidays is quite different. Pentecost has none of the trappings that make Christmas and Easter the two major holidays of the year. Children don't get all excited at the thought that Pentecost is coming. No gifts are exchanged, no decorations hung, no big family gatherings or special meals on Pentecost day. And, as you can see, we do not get the same crowds at church for this feast as we do for Christmas and Easter!

For most people, today is not different in any way from an ordinary Sunday. On the one hand, it is too bad that we don't go all out to celebrate this day, because at the heart of the ritual and imagery of Pentecost lies the reality that gives power to our religious life, that enables us to know God and to enter into union with him. On the other hand, because there is no secular overlap, no extraneous trappings to distract us on this day, we might be able to see more clearly, to enter more fully, into this glorious reality of the very Spirit and love of God that is given to us as gift, to make us alive in God.

The story of our salvation, as we know it from the Bible, is filled with the presence of the Spirit. It is helpful to remember that a single Hebrew word is translated as "wind," "breath," and "spirit," and that their meaning is often interchangeable. In the very first chapter of Genesis, the Spirit of God is hovering over the watery chaos as the creative spirit that will bring form and order where there is none. And in the second chapter, after man is formed from the clay of the earth, God breathes into him the breath of life and man becomes a living being.

The Spirit of God is given to those who are called to lead God's people: to Moses and the elders in the desert, to the charismatic leaders who emerged during the settlement of the promised land, to Saul and to David, to the kings and the priests. The Spirit of God calls individuals to the prophetic task, fills them with burning zeal for the Lord, and sends them forth to speak God's word of challenge, judgment, invitation, comfort, hope. The Spirit guides those who pass on, and interpret, and write down and preserve God's word, God's law, the story of what God has done for his people.

There was a feeling that the Spirit of God, particularly the prophetic Spirit, was no longer visibly active among God's people in the last four hundred years before the coming of Jesus. In the Christian Scriptures, Luke is the author who insists that the Spirit has returned with Jesus and has been given to his Church. The Spirit of God is part of the story of the conception of Jesus, present at his baptism, active in the signs and wonders Jesus performs, promised to those who follow Jesus. And almost every page of the book of the Acts of the Apostles reveals the presence of the Spirit guiding the early Christian communities in the humanly impossible task of proclaiming the Good News of salvation in Jesus Christ to the whole world.

Our three readings today tell us in three different ways of the meaning of the Holy Spirit in our life. In the Gospel, the Risen Christ comes to his disciples to bring them peace and dispel their fears and to commission them to go forth and continue the same mission he had received from the Father. He breathes on them and gives them the gift of the Spirit so that they may bring peace and reconciliation to others. That same Spirit has been given to us in baptism and confirmation. In the same Spirit we are to be the instruments of reconciliation and forgiveness to others.

In the first reading the book of Acts describes with spectacular images and metaphors the first Pentecost. (A recent newspaper article described the celebration of the Jewish feast of Shavuot, which is celebrated fifty days after Passover. Beginning as an early harvest feast, by the time of the book of

Acts this feast had become a memorial of the giving of the Law to Moses on Mount Sinai. The people mentioned in today's reading had come from all over the world to Jerusalem to celebrate this feast.) Filled with the Holy Spirit, the disciples begin to speak in solemn, oracular fashion. Luke was convinced that in this event the ancient curse of separation and division, begun with the confusion of languages at the tower of Babel, was being reversed, and a new age was being inaugurated. People once scattered by the Lord now would be gathered together, and confusion is replaced by understanding. We are part of the new age, and the Spirit is at work in us. Are we ready to make bold proclamation of this possibility of unity and understanding for our world?

Writing to the Corinthians, Paul describes the same ideal of unity in different words. Having been baptized into the one body of Christ by the same Holy Spirit, it does not matter whether we are black or white, female or male, rich or poor. We are all richly gifted by the same Spirit; the differences themselves are gifts to give depth and breadth, richness and variety to God's people. Each of us has different manifestations of the Spirit, not for our own gain or advantage, but for the common good. I think that this is one of the most important truths we can proclaim to our time: that all of us are gifted, and that all of us have something to give, and that our gifts, our talents, our abilities, are not just for ourselves, for our private, individual advantage, but must be used for the common good, for the sake of the human community, if there is to be any hope for humanity.

I recently read about three examples of how people have used their gifts. An eighty-four-year-old woman, a religious for sixty-four years, eleven of them in China, has gone with four others to begin a contemplative convent in Guatemala. They will support themselves and try to be signs of the presence of God in the world, to help others achieve a deeper humanity, by deepening their prayer life, by carrying the world in their hearts as they are lifted to God.

A second example is a man whom *Time* magazine described as one of the smartest people in the world, and whom many think will one day be named to the U.S. Supreme Court. A Harvard graduate, he went to Cambridge, England, for a graduate degree in English and then obtained a law degree from Harvard Law School. He also obtained an M.A. and a Ph.D. in philosophy from Catholic University of America because he felt he needed a better education in Catholic thought and ideas. He says: "I was quite certain that the most important ideas for me were Catholic, and I felt very much that my education had not kept up with my religious life." His books and his teaching at Berkeley have influenced many people.

The final example is a simple story told by Jean Vanier, founder of L'Arche, the movement for housing and working with people with disabilities. A group went on a pilgrimage to the Holy Land.

> When they arrived at the heavily guarded airport in Israel, Jean Claude, one of the handicapped men, walked right up to the Israeli armed soldiers and started to give each one a hand telling them how glad he was to have arrived in the Holy Land. Indeed, very broken people often allow us to see our true selves hidden behind our uniforms and rifles. They tell us that we are really brothers and sisters and that arms and weapons do not tell the truth of who we are.[22]

What story can we tell about our gifts in the Spirit? We all have different gifts, different ministries, different works. How will we use them for the common good? Will we let the Spirit accomplish his purpose in us and through our gifts? What marvelous things the Spirit of God could do if we let him! He could renew the face of the earth!

# At a Loss for Words

TIME: JUNE 2, 1996
SEASON: TRINITY SUNDAY
SCRIPTURE READINGS: EXODUS 34:4B–6, 8–9;
2 CORINTHIANS 13:11–13; JOHN 3:16–18

Blessed are you, O Lord, the God of our fathers, praiseworthy and exalted above all forever; and blessed is your holy and glorious name, praiseworthy and exalted above all for all ages."

These are the words we prayed as the responsorial psalm. They are taken from Daniel 3:52–56, the canticle of the three young men in the fiery furnace, who ended up there because they refused to worship the statue of the king and remained faithful to the God of their fathers. They were saved by an angel sent to protect them. There is a contemporary sound in the ancient story: It is risky, it is dangerous to be truly faithful to God, to refuse to worship the images of power, the promises of glory that our world offers us. But, for us as for those three young men, God is forever faithful. God's love saves us and keeps us alive.

In today's readings, according to one commentator:

> We hear the covenant demands; we stand in awe at the revelation of our God who is loving and faithful. We know the fiery furnace in which we live; we know how hard it is to be faithful in love and peace. But God has sent not an angel but Jesus to deliver us. We borrow the courage of the three men and focus not on our own weakness but the greatness of our God. 'Blessed are you, O Lord!'[23]

Once again we meet the greatness, the holiness of God. How do we talk about the mystery of our God? Where do we find the words to describe the reality that transcends all our images, experiences, encounters, our whole universe? How do we speak of the presence that is more intimate to us than our own very breath and heartbeat, that is deep within, at the core of all that moves and has being?

We have to start by recognizing that we cannot capture the mystery, that all our words will fail us and all our images will fall short. When our mind has done its best thinking, when our imagination has exhausted all its creative powers and we have run out of words, we will have no choice but to stand mute and silent, in awe before the mystery of God.

I am sure you have heard this story about Thomas Aquinas, one of the greatest theological minds in the history of Christianity. Toward the end of his life he had a mystical experience of God, a moment of direct encounter with the glory of God. After that he never wrote another word, and described all he had written as nothing but straw, because he had come to the realization that all his many volumes of profound reasoning about God did not begin to do justice to the mystery of God. He had no words to express what he had come to know in that moment of intimate encounter with the living God. And Thomas Aquinas is the one who repeatedly insists that all our knowledge and our language about God are only analogical. He warns us not to take our reasoning and images about God as the literal truth, as exact representations of the mysterious reality of God. All that we say about God is in some ways appropriate and in some ways inappropriate; in some ways it corresponds to the reality and in some ways it obscures it; in some ways it fits and in some ways it does not.

Another way to approach God is by turning to the historical process through which God has revealed himself to us. In the first reading we have just a hint of a mysterious encounter between Moses and the God of Israel which is a powerful illustration of what I am trying to say. Moses, a little earlier in the story, had asked God: "Show me your glory, I pray" (33:18). Yahweh answered him: "I will make all my goodness pass before you, and I will proclaim before you the name, 'The Lord,' . . . . But you cannot see my face; for no one shall see me and live" (3:19–20). Yahweh tells Moses where to stand and tells him that when God's glory passes by, God will push him in the cleft of the rock and cover him, until God has passed by: "[T]hen I will take away my hand, and you shall see my back; but my face shall not be seen" (32:23). We cannot see God's face, only his back. Next morning Moses does as he had been told, and God indeed comes and describes who God is:

"The Lord, the Lord, a God merciful and gracious, slow to anger, and abounding in steadfast love and faithfulness, keeping steadfast love for the thousandth generation . . . ." (34:6–7a).

I have never seen a study of the number of times this phrase is repeated, but I have the impression that it is one of the descriptions of God found most often in the Bible. Is that not also what today's Gospel reading is saying to us? "God so loved the world that he gave his only son that whoever believes in him may not die but have eternal life" (John 3:16). That is how steadfast God's love for us has been: God has given the world his only Son!

We have just completed the cycle of our liturgical feasts. At Christmas we were filled with wonder and tender feelings as we looked at a newborn child and were told that this was God's Son, that God was a Father, a Parent. During Holy Week we remembered how this man Jesus was faithful to the mission he had received from the Father even unto death, death on a cross, death for our sake. At Easter we rejoiced in the news that the Father had delivered the Son from death and raised him to new life. Last week, at Pentecost, we celebrated the gift of the Spirit of God that makes us alive in the very life of God, both as individual persons and as a community of faith and love.

Today we bring all these titles and images together, and we give praise to God in the great Trinitarian formula: In the name of the Father and of the Son and of the Holy Spirit. Beautiful, enduring, powerful images! But even here we must not forget that these are only analogies, that we cannot think of God as if these words and images were exact parallels of our experiences of parent-child relationships, of human spirit and creative powers. We only need to remember how fragile our relationships are—at times tortured, painful, even destructive. We only need to remember the bloody wars fought by our ancestors in the faith about the meaning of these words and relationships when applied to God. Our deepest point of contention with Greek Orthodox Christians is still two words in the creed that describe the relationship of the Holy Spirit to the Son![24]

What do these words mean to you? How do you understand them? What are your images of God? How do you think of God? Do you ever speak of God? I invite you to take these questions seriously. I wish we had the time, the opportunity to enter into a conversation about this. For me the image of God is one of profound mystery, and the Trinitarian formula speaks to me of relationships in love. Our life is lived so much on the surface, for the moment. To meet the living God I must be willing to go into the depth of my own being, because God is there. God for me is the very depth of my being and of everything that is, the very source of my life, the very goal of my living, the reality that engages my whole self, without reservations or holding back.

The more I know myself, the more I am in touch with who I am at that deepest level, the more I will be able to open myself as person to another person, the more personal "I" will be able to see, to meet, to be united with the personal "thou" of another, and out of this deeply personal encounter a new reality will emerge, the "we" of a unity of persons. I think the more we are able to enter into this kind of deeply personal relationship, the more we will be able to encounter our God, who has revealed the mystery of the divine reality and life as a community of relationships that we have named Father, Son, and Holy Spirit.

O, how we long to see the face of God! Don't you wish you could know God ever more intimately, ever more deeply? Don't you long to encounter the living God, the gracious, merciful, loving God who has revealed himself in Jesus and called us to share the divine life in the Spirit? I believe that this is the built-in desire and longing that has called us to life and that continues to haunt us until, like Moses, like Thomas, we meet the mystery of God in a moment of intimate, overwhelming revelation. And then there will be no more need for words, or images, or concepts. We will be at peace in the mystery, and God will be enough. "Blessed are you, O Lord our God, praiseworthy and exalted above all forever!"

# Sharing Slow Food

TIME: JUNE 17, 1990
SEASON: BODY AND BLOOD OF CHRIST
SCRIPTURE READINGS: DEUTERONOMY 8:2–3,14B–16A;
1 CORINTHIANS 10:16–17; JOHN 6:51–58

The first reading from Deuteronomy gives us one of the versions of the story of manna, the heavenly bread for the desert journey, a gift echoed in the Gospel and still remembered and celebrated today. Manna was mysterious as to where it came from or what it is. The popular etymology of the word is based on a detail of the story in the version found in the book of Exodus, chapter 16. So mystified were the Hebrews when they saw this substance that God had given them for bread, that they said: "Man hu," or "What is this?" (Manna was always just right for the needs of each person. If you picked a lot, you did not end up with too much, and if you picked less, you still had enough. You could not hoard manna. Those who went against Moses' directive, who were afraid that the manna might not come the next day and tried to save some for tomorrow, soon discovered that it immediately smelled bad and bred maggots.)

As the story goes, the Hebrews got manna in the desert for forty years, and from time to time one gets the impression that they grew tired of it. As the story is remembered in today's text, it appears in the context of the interpretation of the whole time of wandering in the desert as a time of testing, to find out if the people would remain faithful to God and his covenant. Through hunger the people are taught to rely on God not only for the physical nourishment of daily bread but also for all forms of nourishment that come from God's creative word, the word that has the power to make new worlds come into existence.

Paul's statement in today's second reading is part of his warning against offering sacrifices to idols. For Paul false gods do not exist, but there are demons behind the worship of idols, and offering sacrifices, participating in ritual meals, are acts that unite the believer to the object of faith. Since the Christian Eucharist is an act of communion with Christ, those who are in communion with him cannot participate in acts that would put them in communion with demons. It is important for us to grasp Paul's understanding, which comes from his Jewish background and becomes part of the Christian tradition: Participation in the sacred meal brings about communion with God in Christ, and also communion, unity among those who share in the meal, just as the many grains of wheat become the one fragrant loaf of bread.

We need to hear Jesus' words in the Gospel with the same sense of shock that was the reaction of his hearers. Jesus is directly confronting deep-seated traditional beliefs, like the repugnance against cannibalism (see Deut. 28:53–57, where it is seen as a curse and one of the unspeakable tragedies of the Babylonian conquest of Judah), and the Torah's strict prohibitions against eating or even touching blood. One commentator explains: "The shock of such sayings is intended to make Jesus' hearers look at things in a new way, with their minds 'blown open,' as it were, to receive new understanding and even new revelation."[25] In the Gospel of John the new revelation is that Jesus is the source of all that really matters in human existence, that he is the link between God and us, that he brings us the possibility of sharing in the very life of God, for he is the way that leads to God and the truth that sets us free and the life that never ends.

Maybe we need to be shocked by hearing as if we had never heard them before the words of Jesus: "He who feeds on my flesh and drinks my blood has life eternal, and I will raise him up on the last day. For my flesh is real food and my blood real drink" (John 6:54–55).[26] Or at least we need to be reminded of the mystery and the greatness and the power of this gift through which Jesus gives himself to us, his whole life and being, his risen humanity and his eternal divinity, his body nailed to the cross and raised from the dead to new life, his blood poured out for the salvation of the world. And he gives himself as gift to us so that we may live in communion with him, so that we may share his life. (When we consume other food, what we take in is transformed into our own body. When we consume the eucharistic bread and wine, we are transformed into him.)

Perhaps it was the experience of communion with the Lord in the Eucharist that moved Paul to say: "It is no longer I who live, but Christ who lives in me" (Gal. 2:20). And St. Augustine reports that he heard Jesus say to him: "I am the food for grown men and women; grow and you shall eat me. And you shall not change me into yourself, the way bodily food acts; you shall be changed into me."[27]

We need to approach the Eucharist with the same wonder of the Hebrews when they first saw the manna, and ask: What is this? What is this mystery, what is this gift, what is this communion with the Lord, this sharing of his life that I am about to receive? And, like the manna, it is not something that I can hoard for myself. Giovanni Papini, one of the great spiritual writers of the first part of the twentieth century, once addressed a satirical letter "To the Monks and Brothers," in which he said: "He who lives in prayer and renunciation to achieve his own salvation is not yet a saint. He is the purest of egotists...."[28] The gift of the Eucharist is also very much for the building of a community of faith, a community that will give of itself in love as bread broken and blood poured out for the hungers and the needs of others, as Jesus did.

At the communal celebration of the first communion of our children I mentioned a new movement that started recently in my part of Italy called *Cucina Lenta,* Slow Cooking. It is a reaction to the fast-food craze that is spreading all over the world. It wants to preserve or recapture the pleasure of eating carefully prepared food in the company of family and friends as a social, relational event that is an essential part of a good human life. Sometimes I think that we approach the Eucharist as if it were a fast-food franchise, looking for the shortest Mass, coming and leaving in a hurry, taking it all in isolation, without paying any attention or saying a word or giving a look to the people who are sharing with us what has been called "the heavenly banquet." I prefer a slow Eucharist, taking my time, lingering over each precious moment, listening to every word, savoring the silences, seeing the faces, looking into the eyes, sharing the holiness, the awe, the joy of this mystery of presence and love with all who have gathered to celebrate the Eucharist together.

# What Are We Doing Here?

Time: June 8, 1975
Season: Tenth Sunday in Ordinary Time
Scripture Readings: Hosea 6:3–6; Romans 4:18–25; Matthew 9:9–13

In today's Gospel, Jesus tells the Pharisees, and us, to learn the meaning of the words of the prophet Hosea, which we heard in our first reading. These must be important words to have survived from the eighth century before Christ. They must be an important part of the religious experience which is shared by Hosea, Jesus, and us.

The Gospel describes a familiar story and situation in the life of Jesus. There is the unexpected call, and perhaps the equally unexpected answer: "Follow me," and Matthew follows him. Then there is the celebration in Matthew's home where Jesus shares food with those who are regarded as sinners. This brings a hostile reaction from the Pharisees, to which Jesus' answer is the words that endure to our time: "It is not sacrifice that I desire but mercy."

I think we would be making a mistake if we were to set up a contrast between sacrifice and ritual on the one side and love, mercy, the knowledge of God on the other. If that were true, then we should all get up from our seats and go home, because that is what we are doing here: This is ritual, a ritual that traditionally has been described as the holy sacrifice of the Mass. So, we should all go home and love. The only problem is that love can be just as empty as ritual can be.

I really don't think there is support in these passages for the attitude that says: "There's no need for me to go to church to be religious." If we look at Hosea's idea in its context, we find that when worship in the Temple is threatened by invading armies, Hosea is very upset. He describes this loss as a tragedy, as a punishment for sin and infidelity. And Jesus himself is involved in going to the Temple, participating in ritual, praying in the Temple. In the ritual setting of the Passover meal, he performs the ritual actions which we will repeat today, which have become our Eucharist, our sacrifice.

It is true, of course, that ritual and sacrifice and going to church on Sunday are not enough by themselves to make a person religious. Unless these acts, and our participation in the ritual and in the sacrifice, are rooted in a life of obedience and mercy and love, then they are empty and without meaning. But the contrast Jesus makes is between the self-righteous and the sinner. If I come to the moment of ritual and worship and sacrifice with an awareness of my own sinfulness, then perhaps I will not be so inclined to take a holier-than-thou attitude that says: "I am better than you are because I go to church every Sunday." And if I have known my own need for God's mercy and forgiveness, then perhaps I will be more inclined to be merciful toward another who injures me.

But how can we go about learning the meaning of the words, "It is mercy, it is love I desire, not sacrifice?" Maybe a story will help. There is a famous novel by Rumer Godden entitled *In This House of Brede,* which was made into a very beautiful television film. It's the story of a successful business woman in the England of our time who becomes weary of people and success and work, the pressures of life in the world, and decides to leave the world and devote her time to prayer and worship and contemplation. She joins a Benedictine convent where the traditional habit is worn and the traditional Benedictine order is observed. There is silence. There is the haunting sound of Gregorian chant echoing through the halls, and it is truly a beautiful setting and a powerful place of prayer. The woman, Dame Margaret, finds an abundance of the peace and union with God that she was seeking.

For several years she goes along in this attitude of prayer and contemplation. But one day, a young novice enters who is in desperate need of love and attention and who seeks out her friendship. Dame Margaret is confronted with the realization that loving God by itself is not sufficient, that it is impossible to love God unless one is also willing to love people. She finds it very easy to love the young novice, who is a likeable person. But Dame Margaret also has to learn the lesson that the love of God calls us to love even those who are not loveable, those who cannot return love, those who return our love with insult. She ends up caring for those who are sick and dying in the infirmary, those who are not even aware of the loving care she is giving them and who cannot respond to it in any way. But even there something extraordinary happens. A nun who had been her bitter critic, her enemy, who had tried to push her out of the convent, dies in the infirmary in Dame Margaret's arms, reconciled and at peace.

"It is mercy I desire, and not sacrifice." It is easy enough to understand the phrase in that kind of setting, in that beautiful story. But what does it mean in our life? What do those words mean to us? Perhaps we need to look at this question: What do we ask from and what do we give to one another in our human relationships?

Husband and wife, what do you exchange? Is it just words, beautiful-sounding words, or is it truly the sharing of love? When you do something for one another, do you have the feeling that you are making a great sacrifice for the sake of the other, or is it an offering of love? When one fails, what does the other one give? Is it mercy and compassion, or is it judgment and condemnation?

Parents and children can be very demanding of one another at times. You know the attitude: "I have made all these sacrifices for you all my life, and now look what you are doing to me," or "Yes, you have loved me, but you have kept me in prison. You have never let me be free. You have demanded of me more than you have given."

What about our situation right here, in a community that wants to call itself Christian? How easy it is to come to church and feel good when there is beautiful music, when we are surrounded by beautiful people, when we participate in a moving liturgy that someone has prepared for us. But how difficult it is to be loving and merciful even toward everyone here, let alone everybody outside in the world. How easy it is to welcome into our community the beautiful, the strong, the healthy, all the dear friends who like us, all those who support us and never make demands on us. What a travesty of the gospel if a

Christian community finds no room and no acceptance for the ugly, the poor, the weak, the sick, those with disabilities, those who dislike us and oppose us, those who trouble us, and those who are so terribly unreasonable in their expectations and demands of us.

Again, what do we ask from the Christian community, and what are we willing to give to it? Do we come looking for a place where we can gather with our friends and be all together in a loving little group and support one another and be comfortable with one another and hear words of comfort and consolation from a preacher who makes us feel good? And what will we give? Our precious presence at Sunday Mass for 60 minutes (and it had better not be 65!)? Our financial support, our treasured words of wisdom and advice? Or are we really willing to give of ourselves? To give of ourselves, whatever we are, whatever we have to offer, and to do it in love and mercy and compassion to whomever needs, whomever asks for our words, our help, our presence, whatever it may be?

To make it very concrete, let me tell you what these texts and this liturgy have done for me. They have forced me to rethink very seriously my own personal attitude toward the refugees from Vietnam who have come to our country and our community.

The Gospel says: "I have come to call not the self-righteous but sinners." How difficult it is to understand the meaning of those words. "It is love and mercy that I desire, not sacrifice." And if it is difficult to understand, how much more difficult it is to live out. And yet, how empty our ritual and our sacrifice will be without this kind of life attitude and life commitment to the same kind of mercy and love for one another which we have experienced ourselves as God's gift in Christ Jesus. May God bless us.

# How Dare You Treat Me That Way!

Time: June 22, 1975
Season: Twelfth Sunday in Ordinary Time
Scripture Readings: Jeremiah 20:10–13; Romans 5:12–15; Matthew 10:26–33

The God of the Judeo-Christian tradition, the God of our faith, is not an absentee landlord. He is not an abstract principle of philosophy or some unnamed impersonal force. Our God is personal, and personal means that which is characteristic of persons, of individuals who are able to act and react to one another. With persons, we can become angry and we can plead. Between persons there is intimate knowledge and profound trust. If God is personal, we must be able to do that with him, too. And this is the way that the readings in today's liturgy speak of God.

The passage from which the first reading is taken is one of the most powerful in the Old Testament, but it doesn't come through, you do not feel all of its strength when you take only four verses out of context. So, I would like to read the whole passage. It's known as Jeremiah's interior crisis. It's a kind of explosion that comes from the prophet out of his anger and fear, doubt and despair, and perhaps even rebellion against God.

The historical circumstances reflected in this passage were that Jeremiah was proclaiming the imminent destruction and exile of the people because of their infidelity, because of their turning to political alliances. Jeremiah was a prophet of doom, and as such he was not very popular. He was seized, he was scourged, and he was placed publicly in stocks. Then he was released, but he continued his prophecy of destruction and exile and again became the object of ridicule and laughter and derision. Even his friends are standing by, waiting for him to fall. And this is what he says (Jer. 20:7–18):

> O Lord, you have enticed me,
>    and I was enticed;
> you have overpowered me,
>    and you have prevailed.

I have become a laughingstock all day long;
> everyone mocks me.
For whenever I speak, I must cry out,
> I must shout, "Violence and destruction!"
For the word of the Lord has become for me
> a reproach and derision all day long.
If I say, "I will not mention him,
> or speak any more in his name,"
then within me there is something like a burning fire
> shut up in my bones;
I am weary with holding it in,
> and I cannot.
For I hear many whispering:
> "Terror is all around!
Denounce him! Let us denounce him!"
> All my close friends are watching for me to stumble.
"Perhaps he can be enticed,
> and we can prevail against him,
> and take our revenge on him."
But the Lord is with me like a dread warrior;
> therefore my persecutors will stumble,
> and they will not prevail.
They will be greatly shamed,
> for they will not succeed.
Their eternal dishonor
> will never be forgotten.
O Lord of hosts, you test the righteous,
> you see the heart and the mind;
let me see your retribution upon them,
> for to you I have committed my cause.
Sing to the Lord;
> praise the Lord!
For he has delivered the life of the needy
> from the hands of evildoers.
Cursed be the day
> on which I was born!
The day when my mother bore me,
> let it not be blessed!
Cursed be the man
> who brought the news to my father, saying,
"A child is born to you, a son,"
> making him very glad.
Let that man be like the cities
> that the Lord overthrew without pity;

> let him hear a cry in the morning
> > and an alarm at noon,
> because he did not kill me in the womb;
> > so my mother would have been my grave,
> > and her womb forever great.
> Why did I come forth from the womb
> > to see toil and sorrow,
> > and spend my days in shame?

There's no doubt about how the prophet is feeling, is there? He is angry at God, and he is hurt that God, having chosen him as prophet, having led him to speak in his name, has led him to this kind of a situation. He wants to turn away from God. He wants to refuse to continue his mission to speak in God's name, but he can't do it. That word is like fire burning in his heart, imprisoned in his bones, and he can't hold it in, he can't endure it. And still, he feels the mockery, especially from the friends who have turned against him. And he shouts, demanding that God be like a mighty champion for him. He even asks for vengeance on his enemies.

There is a word of hope, but then Jeremiah ends with a cry of terrible pessimism and utter despair. He says he would prefer not to have been born. It almost sounds blasphemous, doesn't it? It almost sounds like a man who is turning against God. And yet these are the words of one of the greatest of the prophets, one of the greatest men in the history of the Judeo-Christian religious experience, a man of immense, burning faith for whom God is as real and as present, as immanent and as personal, as the friends who have turned against him. Perhaps more so. And that's why Jeremiah can speak to God that way, because God is real and personal and his friend. And when he feels betrayed, he tells him so. And when he feels abandoned, he cries out to God.

I don't know if you ever feel these kinds of emotions, if you've ever experienced the same kind of reaction to God in your life. If you ever do, you should not be afraid of it. This kind of feeling, this kind of way of dealing with God, is not a rebellion. It's not a denial of faith. Rather, it's the expression of a very deep faith. It's the expression of a person who knows with his or her whole being that God is not some kind of abstraction but a real person who is intimately and immediately present and close to him or her.

It may sound foolish to talk about God as being so personal and so near. Maybe this is just another projection of human beings, another result of human imagination. But on the other hand, Paul, in the Letter to the Romans, tells us that the abundance of God's grace and of God's gracious gifts is in this man Jesus Christ, in this human person who is named Jesus. So that is how God has finally revealed himself to us—in flesh and blood, in a person who is born, who lives a human life, who dies a human death, who lives as a human being with feelings and emotions, with ideas and the ability to act and interact with other human beings. If that is so, then it seems to me that is how God wants us to know him, to think of him, to respond to him: as he was heard and met and spoken to in Jesus Christ.

If our God is personal, how does he answer a cry of despair similar to that of Jeremiah? It seems to me that the Gospel answers Jeremiah's outburst. In the Gospel, Jesus, in very concrete language, tries to convey to us the totality, the absoluteness of God's care for us: "Are not two sparrows sold for a small coin? Yet not one of them falls to the ground without your Father's knowledge. Even all the hairs of your head are counted. So do not be afraid; you are worth more than many sparrows." Sparrows still fall and die, but the Father cares. He cares enough to send his only son who is Jesus Christ. Then we have another hope, another assurance, another answer, based on another promise. Jesus also says that if we acknowledge him before men he will acknowledge us before his Father. And so we have not only the Father but also someone who stands by us, who speaks for us, who intercedes on our behalf: Jesus Christ, our brother. May God bless us.

## Welcoming the Stranger

Time: July 1, 1990
Season: Thirteenth Sunday in Ordinary Time
Scripture Readings: 2 Kings 4:8–11, 14–16a;
   Romans 6:3–4, 8–11; Matthew 10:37–42

Thursday morning, while driving to church for Mass, I heard an interview with Walter Mondale on the radio. The occasion was the apparent willingness of President Bush to consider the need for higher taxes to control and reduce our enormous deficit and national debt. Mondale lost the 1984 presidential election by a landslide—partly, at least, because he said that higher taxes were inevitable and he wanted to be honest about it and tell people what was going to happen. Mondale made a point that stayed with me. He said that political leaders must be willing to talk about the burdens of citizenship.

We hear a lot about the privileges, the rights, the benefits of being an American citizen, but not much about the responsibilities, the duties—yes, the burdens—that go with it. There is a high cost for freedom, for equality, for democracy, for justice, and we have become less and less willing to accept the burden, to pay the cost.

Part of the cost, part of the burden of our democracy, is the difficulty of maintaining a unity of purpose, of vision, of direction, given the multiplicity of cultures, historical backgrounds, religious experiences, and ways of life that make up the mosaic of American society.

Writers and speakers at one time used the image of the melting pot to describe the American situation brought about by the continuing immigration of people from all over the world and their assimilation into American society. That image has been found inadequate, because it implies too much a loss of one's own culture, history, identity, for the sake of the common soup. The image used today is that of the mosaic. How can we fit together all these different pieces, each with its own color and shape and identity, so that together they will form that magnificent picture of a decent human life, with liberty and justice for all, that has been the genius and the vision of American democracy?

The theme of hospitality jumped out at me from the first reading and the Gospel, and I thought of how hospitable this land has been to so many people, beginning with the Native Americans welcoming the Pilgrims, to the latest wave of immigrants and refugees from south of the border and from Indochina. There have been many attempts to cut off the influx and to turn people against the foreigners who have come looking for a better life in this country, but I believe that our hospitality, our willingness to welcome the strangers and the poor who come knocking at our doors, has been unmatched in the history of the world.

I went back to a wonderful book by Henri Nouwen because I remembered that, in talking about the three movements of the spiritual life, he writes about the movement from hostility to hospitality. He begins by saying:

> In our world full of strangers, estranged from their own past, culture and country, from their neighbors, friends and family, from their deepest self and their God we witness a painful search for a hospitable place where life can be lived without fear and where community can be found.[29]

Is this not the refrain we hear so often and from so many different quarters? Growing estrangement and the need for a welcoming, friendly environment. And is this not a major part of our Christian vocation? To create a friendly space for the stranger. Hospitality is one of the richest biblical terms. There is an abundance of stories in the Hebrew and Christian Scriptures that speak of the obligation of hospitality, the duty to welcome, to receive, to care for the stranger out of one's abundance or out of one's poverty. But all the stories also speak of the precious gifts that the strangers are carrying with them, ready to give to a receptive host.

The first reading is a beautiful example. The Shunammite woman invites Elisha the prophet to share her food and her home, and Elisha gives the promise of something she wanted very much: a child. How often a stranger can bring new creativity, new life, new energy into a situation that is stagnant!

Nouwen says that our first step is to become aware of our hostilities, of our fears, of our competitiveness, if we are ever to move toward a hospitality that is willing to offer friendship without binding the guest, to offer freedom to the guest without leaving him or her alone. Nouwen examines three types of relationships from the perspective of hospitality: parents and children, teachers and students, professionals and patients or clients. He finds common elements that I think are equally applicable to our national situation and its mosaic of cultures.

The host must begin with the premise that both host and guest are engaged in a search for human meaning and values. The relationship begins with the willingness and the ability to listen to the other, to trust the other, to value the experience of the other. The host must be willing to receive, as well as to give; to reveal himself or herself as well as to be open to the self-disclosure of the other; to affirm, encourage, and support the other. Nouwen describes the paradox of hospitality, that poverty makes a good host:

> Poverty is the inner disposition that allows us to take away our defenses and convert our enemies into friends. We can only perceive the stranger as an enemy as long as we have something to defend. But when we say, 'Please enter—my house is your house, my joy is your joy, my sadness is your sadness and my life is your life,' we have nothing to defend, since we have nothing to lose but all to give.[30]

The liturgy today invites us to welcome the Word of God, the holy prophet who comes from God, to welcome the Lord. Sometimes the Lord brings a cross for a present; sometimes the prophet turns our life upside down with his presence. But, always, God comes to us in the other. God only comes to us through other human beings, and especially the stranger, the hungry, the thirsty, the homeless, the sick, the prisoner.

I am proud of the history of hospitality of the United States of America, and I am grateful for it because I myself came as a guest, as a stranger. I hope that we will continue, as a nation, to offer true hospitality to those who come seeking refuge, freedom, a better life—beginning with the strangers who are already in our midst. And I pray that our personal and national hospitality will always be biblical hospitality, the kind that offers not only space and material resources, but also friendship and personal support. I pray that the mosaic we are building will turn out to be a glorious picture of what human beings can accomplish when they work together in mutual trust and respect.

## The Ideal of Humility

TIME: JULY 9, 1972
SEASON: FOURTEENTH SUNDAY IN ORDINARY TIME
SCRIPTURE READINGS: ZECHARIAH 9:9–10;
    ROMANS 8:9, 11–13; MATTHEW 11:25–30

What kind of a world do you hope for? The liturgy tells us to expect and to work for a kingdom in which the gentleness of the Lord, not the fear of retaliation, establishes peace. What kind of person do you want to be? The Lord tells us to be like him who is meek, gentle, and humble. Is this really possible? Does it make sense in our world?

How do we deal with the biblical imagery and call to meekness, gentleness, humility? Is it something viable in our time, or is it rather a condition to be realized in some distant future when the world will be radically different from the present situation? I don't mean this as a rhetorical question.

The biblical statement is not at all ambiguous. We heard a short passage from Zechariah on the Messiah, the awaited ruler of Israel. The prophet does not go into questions of right and wrong and the uses of power. Rather, he envisions the savior of the people as one who rules without violence. He calls this savior meek, pictures him riding on a donkey in an age when kings and warriors rode fine horses. The donkey was part of Israel's poor economy. There were brief periods of splendor, as in Solomon's time (1 Kings 10:26–29) or when the last kings of Judah entered the gates of Jerusalem on chariots and horses (Jer. 17:25; 22:4). But the Messiah will not be this kind of king.

In this passage, the Savior king of the future is portrayed as one who will do God's will and put an end to national self-seeking. He will have no part in the wars and revolutions of the monarchy. He will terminate all violence with his kingdom of peace. The prophet says it is for this gentle person to banish the tools of violence, the chariot and the horse and the bow, and proclaim peace forever.

The king and savior of Zechariah's prophecy appeared in Jesus of Nazareth. The identification is not difficult: the sermon on the mountain, the entry into Jerusalem, the invitation we heard in today's Gospel, his passion and death.

Are meekness, gentleness, humility possible today? I mean for everyone, not just for a few chosen saints. I mean for a nation. Are these virtues or weaknesses? Do we really want a meek president? How important is it for us that the United States be the most powerful nation in the world? How much sympathetic response did the recent movie *The Godfather* evoke? I don't mean the scenes of violence, but the attitude that you just don't let anyone get the best of you. Gentle people get run over and trampled to death. The meek are ridiculed and cheated, and everyone takes advantage of them. Changing cultural attitudes may have regarded meekness and gentleness as virtues in women, but not in men.

We are learning more and more that a healthy human condition, for both individuals and groups, involves strength. We oppose oppression and exploitation. We want to fight for the poor, the powerless, for those who, as a result of their weakness, are deprived of a chance for human life and development. Individuals and groups need a strong sense of identity, an awareness of their own power, an image of self-worth, self-confidence.

Are these things incompatible? I don't know. Perhaps only the person who is strong can be meek and gentle. Perhaps meekness and gentleness are virtues only when I have a choice and willingly let myself be taken advantage of, for the sake of others or of an ideal. Perhaps the meek and gentle person is the one who has great power but does not use it against anyone. Jesus was such a person.

Perhaps meekness and gentleness are not for our time. But unless we begin now, unless each of us begins in our daily encounters, will meekness and gentleness ever begin, will they ever become the accepted way of relating to one another? What else can I say to you except point out to you the meek and gentle Jesus. It is he who says to us: "Learn from me, for I am gentle and humble of heart."

## Taking Root in God's Word

TIME: JULY 14, 1996
SEASON: FIFTEENTH SUNDAY IN ORDINARY TIME
SCRIPTURE READINGS: ISAIAH 55:10–11; ROMANS 8:18–23; MATTHEW 13:1–23

There are both a long and a short version of today's Gospel. The reason I read the short version (vs. 1–9) today is not because I like short Masses or because I am in a hurry to leave. I usually read the longer version, because I believe that the word of God is best heard in its full context. The reason I chose the short version today is because biblical scholars tell us that the portion I read was probably the original parable as spoken by Jesus.

The long version, on the other hand, is an excellent passage for illustrating how, in the canonical texts of the Gospels, there are three main layers of material. First, we have the original sayings or stories from the life and teaching of Jesus. Second, we have the interpretation of those stories by the early Christian community as it began to reflect in faith on its memories of Jesus and to proclaim to others the Good News of salvation in Christ. Third, we have the work of the evangelist, the writer who collected the material, selected what he wanted to use, and arranged it according to his own particular theological vision.

This is not just a theory proposed by Scripture scholars. The Pontifical Biblical Commission, the group in Rome that gives us the official pronouncements of the Church in matters concerning the Bible, in 1964 issued a declaration in which it said that recognizing these three layers, these three stages in the development of the Gospels, is essential to their interpretation and understanding. We will take a little time to look at these three moments in the development of the Gospels.

What was Jesus trying to say in the parable as I read it? He was trying to build up the confidence of the disciples, to give them courage and hope in the face of the incomprehension, suspicion, and hostility that Jesus and the disciples were encountering. In the parable, Jesus describes the random nature of spring planting in his time, when the seed was spread by hand and some fell on the footpaths; some was eaten by birds; some died in rocky, shallow ground; some was choked by weeds. In spite of that, the seed still had yields of 30-, 60-, 100-fold. With this simple and spare image, Jesus is saying: God's rule will be God's doing, and nothing can stop it. In spite of how precarious things look at the beginning, there will be a harvest. He is saying to the disciples: Do not be afraid. God is in charge. The kingdom will come. God's rule will triumph.

The next material, verses 10 to 17, is the attempt of the evangelists, the Gospel writers, to ask and answer the question: Why did Jesus speak so much in parables? The original quotation from Isaiah 6:9–10 reflected the prophet's heavy irony as he confronted the stubbornness, the hardness of heart of his listeners. The Gospel writers interpret the words literally, "probably because they were so set back at the nonacceptance of their proclamation of the crucified and risen Christ that they needed a biblical explanation of it."[31] They found it in this passage that seems to say that the people's hardness of heart is part of God's plan. Those verses give us the third stage of the development of the Gospels, i.e., the theological interpretation of the Gospel writers.

The last group of verses (18–23) gives us the interpretation of the original parable by the early Christian community, as they were beginning to experience different levels of sincerity and commitment, of fidelity and obedience to the proclamation of Jesus as the Savior of the world, as the Messiah promised by God, as the new Moses, as the very personal presence of the gracious and compassionate God in their midst. The original fervor and enthusiasm were beginning to wane. In this situation the faith of the Christian community adapts the parable to the individual believer: The seed becomes the word of God, and the different outcomes of the planting now depend on the disposition of the listener and believer. Only those who really listen and believe, only those who let the word of God sink deep within them, only those who nurture and treasure that word, will bring forth abundant fruit.

I encourage you to read the entire passage from Matthew. Is all this just an exercise in speculation, something perhaps of interest to scholars and seminary students, but of no use to the people in the pews, who are looking for simple but solid nourishment? I hope not. I hope we can glimpse the richness and the power of the word of God when we are able to see it and understand it in its original setting and meaning. Because all this material remains the word of God; all three layers are now canonical Gospel, the very foundation and touchstone of our faith.

How do we hear and interpret the proclamation of the word of God today? The word of God speaks to us in a very personal way, and we need to be attentive to what God is saying to each of us. But the word of God also speaks to us as a community of faith. Today it speaks to us of courage and hope. It dispels our fears and our doubts about the reign of God in our world. Sometimes it is difficult to see where the kingdom of God manifests itself, where it is being realized. Our world does not seem to reflect the values of the kingdom, the values of the gospel. In a recent address before the House of Delegates of the American Medical Association, Cardinal Bernardin of Chicago enumerated what he sees as the major elements of the moral crisis of our society:

> My list includes the shift from family and community to the individual as the primary unit of society, an overemphasis on individual self-interest to the neglect of the common good, the loss of a sense of personal responsibility and the unseemly flight to the refuge of 'victimhood,' the loss of confidence in established institutions, the decline in religious faith, the commercialization of our national existence, the growing reliance on the legal system to redress personal conflicts.[32]

I agree with Cardinal Bernardin's list. I see these problems in our society and in myself. The crisis is not just "out there" someplace. It is in all of us. It affects the Church, our communities, our own personal life. Even so, the Gospel tells us, we should not be afraid, we must not despair, because it is God's kingdom, and although God works in and through us, ultimately it is God's work, God's reign, and God will bring it forth in abundance. The reading from Romans reinforces this

hope. Paul, in the midst of his trials and troubles, is able to say: "I consider that the sufferings of this present time are as nothing compared with the glory to be revealed for us." Paul sees the whole of creation groaning and in agony, in the process of giving birth, and what is being born is the fullness of God's kingdom.

Today's Scripture readings also challenge all of us to look at our heart, to see how we receive the life-giving word of God and what we do with it, whether we allow it to grow in us and to bear fruit. There is hardness and resistance in all our hearts. The word of God is challenging and demanding. It is like a double-edged sword that at times cuts and wounds. We begin to face the challenge by looking at how much time we spend reading the Bible—listening to, reflecting on, praying the word of God. The word of God cannot bear fruit in us unless we allow it to enter into us, to sink roots deep in us, to grow in the silence of our heart, and to bring forth the fruits of compassion and justice, of love and peace, of patience and fidelity, of self-control and obedience.

Isaiah, in the first reading, speaks lyrically, poetically, of the power of God's word that comes forth like a seed, with the power to give life and to nourish, and returns to God having accomplished its purpose. Isaiah is speaking of the prophetic word that God entrusted to the prophets. But we have an even greater, more powerful, life-giving, transforming word: We have Jesus, the Eternal Word of God who became flesh and dwelt among us. We have not just words, we have the living Word, who was with God and is God, who is with us as God's personal presence, right here and now, in this very liturgy. And one of the privileged places where we encounter this living, personal word is in the Scriptures, in the Gospels, in all their richness and variety, in all their layers and stages of development. When we receive the word of God and make it our own, we receive the Lord himself, and we make him our own, just as we receive Jesus and make him our own in the eucharistic memorial we now celebrate.

# Weeds in Our Gardens

Time: July 21, 1996
Season: Sixteenth Sunday in Ordinary Time
Scripture Readings: Wisdom 12:13, 16–19;
  Romans 8:26–27; Matthew 13:24–43

I am not a gardener. I love to be in a beautiful garden, but I prefer to sit in the shade, reading a good book, rather than working in the dirt. I have very little experience with weeds. Right now, in my back yard, I have a couple of ugly-looking things that are growing bigger and bigger, and I don't know what they are. I think they are weeds, but the hired gardener who comes every two weeks to do a little work has not pulled them out, so I figure that either they are some kind of flower or he does not know what they are either. I have been tempted to pull them up, but after reflecting on today's Gospel I am going to let them be. How about you who do love to garden: Do you sometimes have trouble seeing the difference between good plants and weeds?

In the situation described by Jesus, it was very difficult to distinguish between good wheat and something called *darnel*, at least until the wheat was ready to be harvested, when they could be separated. In the parable, Jesus uses the story to tell his disciples that they have to be patient and willing to wait. The reign of God that Jesus has come to establish is not going to be all neat and tidy, all shiny and perfect. The reign of God, in fact, is going to be a messy affair. It is going to have both good and bad in it, light and shadows, people who will bear good fruit and people who look good but are empty and useless. There will even be enemies who will try to sabotage and derail the kingdom of God from the path that God has in mind. The problem is that it is going to be very difficult to tell them apart, the good from the bad, the genuine from the phony. Only God really knows which is which, the God who is able to search the hearts, as Paul reminds us.

Fortunately, the God of our biblical traditions, the God of our Lord Jesus Christ, is a patient God, as we heard in the reading from the book of Wisdom. Our God does not have to prove his might, to parade his power. Here is another translation of the text from Wisdom:

> Although you are sovereign in strength,
> > you judge with mildness,
> > and with great forbearance you govern us;
> > for you have power to act whenever you choose.
> Through such works you have taught your people
> > that the righteous must be kind.
> And you have filled your children with good hope,
> > because you give repentance for sins.

Are you not profoundly grateful that our God governs with great forbearance and judges with mildness? I am! I wonder why the righteous, those who think they are good, those who know they are the good wheat, are so quick to judge and often so harsh in judging others, so ready to condemn those whom they judge to be evil, even before God's judgment is revealed! I must confess that I am very uncomfortable when I hear threats of excommunication and exclusion from the sacraments of our encounter with God, and other attempts to uproot what looks or behaves differently from what we think is right and proper. When we do that we usurp God's prerogative, we claim for ourselves the judgment that belongs to God alone.

Why is it so easy for us to see all that is wrong with those who disagree with us, or who act differently from us? Why do we have such a terrible time recognizing the good that is in another person or group or organization? Why is it that political campaign strategists are so sure that, in order to win an election, candidates have to do everything in their power to destroy their opponents' reputations and discredit them?

The main point I want to make today is this: God looks for and sees the good, not the evil. If you look at the way Jesus acted during his earthly life, and if you believe that his teaching and ministry reflect the way God deals with us, you will see, beyond the shadow of a doubt, that Jesus looks for the good in people, recognizes what is of value in a person, protects sinners from the scorn and threats of the righteous

and empowers them to go beyond whatever evil is in them to live a new life.

Think of Matthew and Zacchaeus, who were tax collectors, the most despised of public figures. Remember the woman who was caught in adultery; too bad the man was not also brought to Jesus. He too could have experienced forgiveness and a new start in life. Try to put yourself in the place of the notorious prostitute, who crashes an elegant dinner party at the home of a leading Pharisee to wash Jesus' feet, who hears Jesus say to his host: "Much is forgiven her, because she has loved much." Remember Peter, who was ready to die for Christ but at the first crisis swears up and down that he does not know him.

This is the way I understand the judgment of God: as a patience that waits and endures the turmoil of the world; that gently works to lead, to persuade the world, and each one of us, by his vision of truth, beauty, and goodness; as a tenderness that looks for what is worth keeping and loses nothing that can be saved; as a wisdom that uses what we would see as mere wreckage.

About a month ago when I was on retreat, the presider at one of the eucharistic liturgies was a Jesuit from Brooklyn who had spent many years in prison ministry. He told the story of a young man, now 24, who committed murder at 19. The young man had been part of a gang but was trying to get out of the gang. He was working in a gas station and planning to be married. But someone from his past, from the underworld, put heavy pressure on him to kill a man. He did it and was caught. He did not deny his guilt, and he got a long prison sentence. When the priest started to minister to him, he was like a dead man—without hopes, without dreams. After awhile the priest suggested to him that at night, in his cell, he try to imagine that Jesus was coming to visit him. It took the man a long time before he could let Jesus into his cell. It took him even longer to get the courage to lift up his head and to look at Jesus, who was looking at him. When he did, he was radically changed, because he saw Jesus looking at the goodness that was in him, in spite of his past. He became a great help to the priest in reaching out to other prisoners, in helping them turn their lives around, by recognizing that there was goodness in them, that they could build a new life on that goodness.

I am sure many of you have seen the film *Dead Man Walking*. Is that not the same thing Sister Helen Prejean was doing with the man condemned to death? She kept looking for a moment of grace, a remnant of decency and goodness, for the condemned man to open himself to the patient, merciful, tender God, and find repentance.

What do you see when you look at the face of an accused man or woman staring at you from a front-page photograph? What do you see in the juveniles who are so often the main characters in stories of violence, drive-by shootings, drug dealing? What do you think when you see all the negative political ads on television? How do you feel about the different groups in the Church that are clashing with one another over questions of dogma, styles of worship, power, authority, control in the institutional Church? What do you see when you look into the face, into the eyes of someone who has hurt you deeply, someone who has disappointed you, perhaps deceived you and betrayed you? How do you feel when you hear stories and discussions and all kinds of categorical statements about immigrants—legal and illegal, about different groups of refugees and exiles whom the political decisions of the powerful and the vagaries of history have brought to our community?

I believe the teaching of the word of God, as we heard it proclaimed today, is not only that we must leave the judgment to God, but also that we must imitate God's judgment and look for what is worthwhile and worth keeping, for what can be saved, for the goodness that is in us, the goodness that God can touch and bring forth in all of us. For that is how God will build us into his kingdom on Earth.

## Make a Wish

TIME: JULY 26, 1987
SEASON: SEVENTEENTH SUNDAY IN ORDINARY TIME
SCRIPTURE READINGS: 1 KINGS 3:5, 7–12; ROMANS 8:28–30; MATTHEW 13:44–52

The world's literature is full of stories like the one we heard in the first reading. The hero (or heroine) of the story meets some sort of supernatural figure who has the power to grant every wish, and he is told to express his one greatest wish. Can you do a little daydreaming and imagine yourself in that kind of situation?

Imagine that the Lord comes to you as he did to Solomon and tells you: "Ask something of me and I will give it to you!" What would you ask? What is your single greatest wish? Remember, it will be granted, and you are going to have to live with it. Be aware of the possible consequences of your choice for yourself and for others! Remember Dostoevsky's saying, so loved and often quoted by Dorothy Day: "Love in action is a harsh and dreadful thing compared to love in dreams."

God is pleased with Solomon's choice because he does not seek wealth, but asks for the skills that will enable him to do well the task to which God has called him, to rule over God's people. Even before God grants the prayer, Solomon appears wise: He understands that faithful service, not selfishness, honors God and brings fulfillment to human life. Solomon gives evidence of a single-minded desire to serve God and God's people.

That is what the Gospel passage describes as the treasure found in the field, as the one really valuable pearl. The Gospel of Matthew generally alternates between narrative sections that describe what Jesus did and discourse sections that contain the speeches of Jesus. The thirteenth chapter, from which we have been reading for several Sundays, is one of the speech sections. In this chapter, the author has collected a number of parables, all of them on the theme of the reign or kingship of God, which is presented as a plan hidden in God and only incompletely manifested to the world (10–17, 34, 44). The teaching of Jesus reveals that it is God who introduces his reign into history (3–9), slowly brings it to fruition through his power (31ff.), and will perfect it in his own good time (24–30).

There is a secondary theme running through this chapter, addressed to the disciples as individuals, encouraging each one to remain faithful to the teachings of Jesus, despite the hardships of rejection and persecution (18–23), to wait patiently for God's own time of resolution of the conflict between good and evil (36–43, 47–50). The kingdom of God, proclaimed and begun in Jesus, is the greatest reality, more valuable than everything else that people hold dear and precious.

Now let's go back for a moment to our daydreaming. What did we ask the Lord to give us? What does our choice say about our values and priorities? Do we feel that the Lord is pleased with our choice, as he was with Solomon's request? In some way our first priority, our highest value, must be connected with God's rule, God's kingdom, God's will. As disciples we are called to make the same choice as the men in today's Gospel: The kingdom of God is the buried treasure, the pearl of great price, and we must be willing to sell everything else to possess it, to be part of it. It is not an easy choice to make. It is not an on-again, off-again situation. It is a life choice; it is total commitment. As someone said: It is so easy for Christians to be saved on Sunday and then be condemned for what they do on Monday. We need to look at our daily life to see if it is consistent with the values we affirm on Sunday, with the choices we profess to make as Christians.

What does the kingdom of God mean in the concrete circumstances of our daily living? There are so many different ways of expressing this mystery, of trying to understand the will of God, the rule of God in our life. I have been reading a book by Richard J. Foster, *Freedom of Simplicity*. As a matter of fact, the entire pastoral staff has been reading this book, and we hope to find some ways of sharing its challenging insights with you, perhaps in Advent and Lent. For some reason the ideal of simplicity of life speaks very strongly and insistently to me, to the place I find myself in my spiritual life at this time. I feel that God's will for me, his rule in my life, is expressed in this vision. It's not easy to talk about simplicity, and it is even more difficult to live it.

On my last priest's retreat the retreat master described simplicity of life in this way: You use what you need and you leave the rest for your brothers and sisters. Pope John XXIII declared: "The older I grow the more clearly I perceive the dignity and winning beauty of simplicity in thought, conduct, and speech, a desire to simplify everything that is complicated, and to treat everything with the greatest naturalness and clarity."[33]

Foster writes about simplicity as living constantly out of a center that gives unity, focus, integration, peace, contentment, to everything that we do, that guides every choice that we make. And that center is God. T. S. Eliot speaks of Christianity as "A condition of complete simplicity (costing us no less than everything)."[34] And a French spiritual writer, François Fénelon, put it most emphatically: "Oh, how amiable this simplicity is! Who will give it to me? I leave all for this. It is the pearl of the Gospel."[35] The pearl of great price. How many of us would ask the Lord for simplicity of life, if we could have anything we wanted?

# Sharing Our Gifts

Time: August 5, 1990
Season: Eighteenth Sunday in Ordinary Time
Scripture Readings: Isaiah 55:1–3; Romans 8:35, 37–39; Matthew 14:13–21

There is a richness, a beauty, a joy in today's Scripture readings that is seldom found in the liturgy for an ordinary Sunday in summer. The word calls us to eat and drink freely, to experience life in its fullness. Our God is a lavish God, fulfilling promises, rescuing us, sticking to us through thick and thin. He can even take the little we have and turn it into an abundant gift for others.

The first reading is an echo of the great Easter Vigil liturgy. This passage from Isaiah was proclaimed then in a longer version. The liturgy of the word in the Easter Vigil is a summary of the story of God's loving relationship with his people. This passage is a reference to the Babylonian exile, not to the tragedy of it, but to the hope and promise of returning home to rebuild the temple, the city, the nation. The verses we heard today assure the captive Israelites that God will come to their rescue.

As the chapter continues, it becomes clear that God's redemption is not only for Israel but for all humanity, even for the whole earth. The prophet invites everyone who thirsts to come to the water and everyone to buy grain, even if they have no money. "God's gifts are given freely and without cost; no one who accepts the invitation to 'come' will be excluded from the people of God."[36] And God provides not only the necessities—water and bread, but also the amenities of milk and wine.

The second reading, from Paul's Letter to the Romans, is for me one of the most beautiful and powerful passages in the Scriptures. In the midst of suffering and hardships, Paul has written an extravagant statement of hope and trust in God. There is no question in Paul's mind that God is faithful to us, that in his love he will hold fast to us. There is nothing, no one, no power in heaven or on earth that can separate us from the love of God, the love he has shown us in Jesus Christ our Lord.

The invitation of Isaiah to come and eat and be satisfied is fulfilled in a new and most unexpected way in the story of the feeding of the multitude. But this is more than just a moment of fulfillment. It is also a moment of foreshadowing and promise of another banquet at which the multitudes will be fed by God's generous love, i.e., the Eucharist. This episode was so important to the earliest Christian communities that there are six different versions of the event in the Gospels. All the accounts have eucharistic overtones.

Today's version follows the announcement of the death of John the Baptist, a foreshadowing of Jesus' own passion and death ritually preserved in the Eucharist. In Matthew, although we first hear of bread and fish, Jesus gives only the bread to the disciples to distribute. The language used to describe Jesus' action is the same as that found in the descriptions of the Last Supper, language that is still repeated in every Eucharist: Jesus takes the bread, blesses it, breaks it, and gives it to the disciples. Both the multiplication of the loaves and the Eucharist are examples of divine bounty and generosity. With the Lord there is always plenty: plenty to eat, plenty to share if we are willing to give him what we have, plenty left over. The Lord's promises are fulfilled: Sickness is healed, hunger is sated, thirst is quenched.

The texts today remind us of the riches that we have received from God: riches of material things, of relationships; riches of faith, of love. What are we going to do with these riches? We are called to follow the model of God: Just as he shared his riches with us, we are called to share our riches with others. What riches do we have to share?

First of all, we have a splendid story to tell, the story of God's parental care for his people, for us. It is a story filled with fantastic characters, stretching back to the very dawn of creation, running through the lives of many faithful servants and the history of a chosen people, coming to a climax in the life, death and resurrection of Jesus, and continuing even to our own time, in the teachings and traditions, in the rituals and celebrations of the Church, but especially in us who have been called by baptism to be God's holy people in the world. Like all great stories, the story of God's love for his creation is not finished; it is still being written in us, in our history. Do we ever share this story of God's love with one another, with our families and friends, with anyone who is willing to listen, with anyone who asks?

Second, we have the abundance, the richness of our eucharistic banquet. Jesus, the Risen Lord, is here in our midst, present in the assembly gathered in his name, in the word proclaimed, in the ministers, in the bread and wine. He is here taking, blessing, breaking and giving the bread of joy and salvation, the bread that continues to feed great multitudes, the bread that gives life. Do we encourage one another to share in the Eucharist? Do we invite others to come? Have you ever invited a friend, a Christian of another denomination, to come and worship with you? Personally, I think it is unfortunate that the Catholic Church officially is so adamant about not sharing the Eucharist with our non-Catholic sisters and brothers. I think that sharing the Eucharist with someone who shares our faith in Jesus Christ and in his eucharistic presence would be a powerful gesture for the building of the unity of Christians for which we all pray and hope.

Finally, we have material riches to share with those who are hungry and thirsty and homeless and old and sick. I recently read a story that I would like to share with you:

> The central committee of the World Council of Churches was meeting in our town. Every church invited a guest to preach. We did not recognize the older man who came to us. He was Welsh; his name was Elfan Rees. All we knew of him was that he had spent much of his life working through the United Nations to help refugees. He knew much about food and drink—not only about celestial banquets but about earthly starvation.
>
> He spoke to us of the hunger he had seen. Then he recalled Christ feeding the thousands. The disciples suggested Christ send the people away to buy food for themselves. Christ told them no. The disciples responded, 'We have only five loaves and two fish here.'

The old man looked around at the gathered people there in Rochester, New York, in the United States. Then he said, with love and sadness, 'That, if you will permit me to say, my dear American friends, is not your problem.'

Then he sat down and a great silence came on us all.[37]

May our sharing in the Eucharist be a sign not only of our eagerness to accept God's generous love but also of our willingness to share with him our loaves and fish for the sake of the hungry multitudes.

# The Sound of Silence

TIME: AUGUST 9, 1987
SEASON: NINETEENTH SUNDAY IN ORDINARY TIME
SCRIPTURE READINGS: 1 KINGS 19:9A, 11–13A;
  ROMANS 9:1–5; MATTHEW 14:22–23

Elijah exercised his prophetic ministry during troubled times in Israel. King Ahab had married a pagan, Jezebel, and allowed her to establish the worship of her Baal gods. Yahweh's own shrines were taken over, his altars toppled, the worship of the true God taken over by idolatry. Elijah had been successful in his confrontation with the priests of Baal. He had prayed to God and called down fire from heaven to consume the altar and the victim of the sacrifice, which the priests of Baal had failed to do, and then summarily executed all 450 of them. This only enraged Jezebel, who swore that she would put Elijah to death. And so he ran for his life into the desert.

Elijah was weary of his struggle, and he prayed for death. His work seemed to be a failure, since he was no more successful than his ancestors in uprooting idolatry, and he began to doubt his ministry and the Lord's presence in his life. But the Lord sustained him with bread and water through a long desert trip to Mount Horeb. There, where God had revealed himself to Moses, Elijah sought the reassurance that God was with him. He even sought the same signs of God's presence: wind, earthquake, and fire. All these signs appear, but God is not there. To Elijah, God reveals himself in "a tiny whispering sound." A more precise translation would be "the voice of silence," meaning an absolute stillness. It is then that Elijah stands and covers his face, for he is in the presence of God. The God who once appeared in the storm now reveals himself in the stillness that follows the storm: God is with the prophet and with his people, but in a new and different way.

In the Gospel, God comes to the disciples in the human person of Jesus, out of the eye of the storm, and they confess him as Son of God in the quiet that follows the storm.

Matthew is the only one of the evangelists to give the vignette of Peter's enthusiasm and failure. For Matthew, Peter is typical of all disciples: He starts out with great courage, but when his faith is put to the test he falters and sinks. He is full of daring, but the raging winds of the storm are stronger than the power of his faith. But he has enough faith to cry out for help to Jesus, whom he calls Lord, and to be caught by his outstretched hand.

Jesus calls Peter "you of little faith." This is a phrase used almost exclusively by Matthew in reference to the disciples. It is really a gentle word, not one of rebuke, that Jesus uses to describe his followers. They are believers, but their faith is just not strong enough yet, and in moments of panic they act as if they did not believe.[38]

I have two questions for our prayer and reflection today: How strong is our faith? Where do we go to find God?

I suspect that Matthew's description of the disciples in his community applies to us as well: Most of us have too little faith. We start out with great conviction and courage and enthusiasm in all our spiritual activities and efforts, but when difficulties arise and the struggle becomes tough, we become afraid and we pull back and sink back into our old ways. How many times have we started to work seriously on our prayer life, resolving to be disciplined in giving proper time to the Lord? And how many times have we allowed other worries and pressures, or a lack of results in prayer, to defeat our original intent? How many times have we been moved by the ideal of simplicity and poverty proclaimed by the Gospel as a way of life for the disciples, and even begun to move in that direction, and then pulled back because it seemed so difficult, because we were afraid? Not only has this happened in the past, but I am sure that this kind of experience will also repeat itself in the future.

The figure of Peter sinking in the waters should give us comfort: This is part of our human weakness. But we also need to learn from Peter, when we find ourselves becoming afraid and pulling back and giving up, to have enough faith at least to cry out to the Lord, to recognize our weakness and to ask him to reach out to us and keep us going.

Where do we go to find God? I suspect that we would all have very similar answers, but each one shaped by our own particular personality and faith history. We all gather here seeking God through the liturgy, as a community, supporting one another, becoming for one another signs of God's presence. Someone put it very well:

> For this reason I need you at worship: Your presence is important, not simply for the health of *your* soul, but also for the health of mine. Your songs, prayers and participation in Christ's body feed me as well as you: my faith is nurtured in seeing your faith. You may not need the nourishment of worship on a given day: but *I* might need your witness at worship desperately. I may need to hear your song and prayers to feed my hungry faith and to strengthen my weak and weary heart.[39]

I am absolutely convinced that we also need to seek God in the quiet stillness of our mind and heart in personal prayer. Communal worship is not enough for a healthy spiritual life, for a growing relationship with God in Jesus Christ. Yes, we can expect to meet God in the storms of our life, when the winds are blowing everything away and the very foundations of our life seem to be shaking. But are we prepared to meet the Lord God in the voice of silence, in absolute stillness and emptiness and nothingness? He is there, too, not the God of favors and miracles, not the God whom we want because of our need, but the living God in the immensity of his being and power, the living God who calls us to enter into the very mystery of his life and love.

## Christian Inclusiveness

TIME: AUGUST 18, 1996
SEASON: TWENTIETH SUNDAY IN ORDINARY TIME
SCRIPTURE READINGS: ISAIAH 56:1, 6–7;
  ROMANS 11:13–15, 29–32; MATTHEW 15:21–28

In the second chapter of the Gospel of Luke we are told twice that the child Jesus grew and became strong, increased in wisdom and in years, and the favor of God was with him. In the same chapter, in the story of the twelve-year-old Jesus who stayed behind in Jerusalem after his parents had left, we read that he was found "in the temple, sitting among the teachers, listening to them and asking them questions. And all who heard him were amazed at his understanding and his answers (Luke 2:46–47).

In the beautiful christological hymn in Philippians, the early Christian community proclaims its faith in the divinity of Jesus, but also in his humanity: He did not hang onto his equality with God, but emptied himself, taking the form of a slave, being born in human likeness, one like us in all things but sin (Phil. 2:6–7). The Letter to the Hebrews insists that, though Jesus is the Son of God, we do have a high priest who is able to sympathize with our weakness, because he was tested in every way that we are, but never sinned (Heb. 4:15). And even Jesus had to learn obedience through suffering (Heb. 5:8).

Through texts such as these, and many others, the Christian Scriptures make it very clear that Jesus is human in every way that we are, except that he did not sin. Do we really believe this? Every time we say the Creed we say explicitly that Jesus became man, that he is human just as we are, while at the same time being the Eternal Word, the Son of God. But are we really convinced of this in our hearts? Do we feel in the core of our own being that Jesus is truly human, with everything that is implied by that word, or is the humanity of Jesus so obscured by the glory of his divinity that we overlook it and minimize it?

My first catechetical and theological education focused on the divinity of Jesus to the point that there was not much room in my faith at that time for the fullness of humanity to be discovered and recognized in Jesus. I am sure that those of you who are around my age had the same experience. It is extremely difficult to keep these two dimensions of the reality of Jesus in balance—his humanity and his divinity. It is a mystery, and there is no parallel to that reality in all of our experience. But we seriously diminish the mystery of Christ, we impoverish our relationship with him, if we overlook either his humanity or his divinity.

Today the Gospel reading invites us to reflect on the humanity of Jesus. If we believe that Jesus is human as we are, in every way except sin, we have to accept the fact that Jesus developed, grew, learned—perhaps even learned from his mistakes—just as we do. Jesus had some extraordinary insights and intuitions about people and situations, but the Gospels also suggest that Jesus, as a human being, did not know everything, that he learned and was enriched by his encounters with people. His vision of himself and his mission was expanded and enlarged by the challenges he met.

This is what happened in the story told in today's Gospel, which is also found, with some variations, in the Gospel of Mark (7:24–30). The story presents a strange and challenging portrayal of Jesus. The woman who comes to ask Jesus for healing for her daughter is not a Jew. She is an outsider to the people of Jesus. My first reaction to the story is to side with the Canaanite woman and wonder why Jesus treats her as he does—first ignoring her, then implying that he was not sent to anyone but the Jews, and finally referring to non-Jews as "dogs."

What is going on in this story? Traditionally, we would have said that Jesus was merely testing the woman's faith, because we wanted to safeguard the divine dimension in Jesus and to affirm that Jesus knew everything, just as God does. In that version, Jesus already knew what he was going to do, but he played a little game with the Canaanite woman. But, if we can step back from that interpretation for a moment, and from the need to protect the omniscience of Jesus, and let the story stand on its own merit and speak to us as it stands in its starkness and ambiguity, then we see that the story is telling us that in this encounter Jesus was challenged to take a second look at his own understanding of his mission, and that he learned some things from a Gentile woman.

When Jesus says that his mission, as Messiah, is only to the lost sheep of the house of Israel, he stands solidly in the traditional expectations of his time. There are echoes of this perception throughout the Gospels. But we also find very clear, overpowering evidence that God's salvation in Jesus Christ is for the whole world, for the nations as well as for the Jews. Through an encounter such as the one described in today's Gospel, Jesus' human consciousness of his own identity, his human understanding of the mission that the Father has entrusted to him, is clarified, expanded, and stretched so that it can embrace the whole world. This moment of growth in understanding and knowledge comes through the insistence, the stubbornness, and the trust of a woman, a mother, who does not give up, because she desperately wants healing for her daughter.

The Canaanite woman refuses to accept that God's salvation, being revealed in Jesus, is limited to Jews. She refuses to believe that she and her daughter are excluded from God's love and compassion by an accident of birth, because they do not belong to the correct religious tradition. She comes to Jesus with an irresistible faith, a faith that is not a doctrinal confession of his divinity or messianic title, or an appeal to his miraculous powers, "but rather an act of trust, of engagement, risking everything. That act has the effect, as the story is told, of enabling Jesus to see the situation in a different way. That new perspective appears to free Jesus to respond, to heal, to become again the channel of God's redeeming presence in that situation."[40]

Jesus learned to be inclusive through his encounter with the Canaanite woman. The human Jesus learned that the mercy and compassion of our gracious God are not limited by any barriers of nationality, race, ethnicity, language, or culture. It is a lesson we also desperately need to learn. The same lesson is proclaimed by Isaiah in the first reading: God's house is a house of prayer for all peoples; no one is excluded. The same lesson is proclaimed in the Letter to the Romans. In chapters 9, 10, and 11, Paul struggles with great pain and agony over the fact that his fellow Jews, by and large, have not accepted the Good News of salvation in Jesus. Why? Paul asks, but he cannot find an answer. He concludes with a magnificent passage in which he expresses his conviction that, somehow, what has happened has the purpose of teaching us that all of us are imprisoned in disobedience and sin, all of us need to experience God's mercy. But God's gifts and his call are irrevocable. God has not taken away his love and his covenant from the Jews. They are still his special people, his beloved children.

Can we learn this lesson? We heard a great deal about "inclusion" in political convention speeches this past week. I hope I am not being too cynical when I say that I felt that the purpose of that reaching out to include everyone was to build up a political party and to gain votes in the November election. The purpose of our call to be inclusive—to embrace, to welcome, to reach out to everyone—goes much deeper. Our purpose is to share the Good News of God's salvation and the gift of his love.

If there is anyone in our experience, any individual or group, any nation or category of people whom we are inclined to look upon as "dogs," as outsiders and strangers, as inferior to us, as not worthy to share in what we have to offer, then we must listen to the challenge of today's biblical message. The challenge is to listen, as Jesus did, to the ones who we think should be excluded, to listen to those who come to us in need, to the poor and the marginalized. We can learn from them the meaning of God's kingdom, the breadth of God's love, the power of God's will to save, to heal, to make one: It embraces even those whom we would rather not recognize as our own.

## For Better and for Worse

TIME: AUGUST 26, 1990
SEASON: TWENTY-FIRST SUNDAY IN ORDINARY TIME
SCRIPTURE READINGS: ISAIAH 22:19–23; ROMANS 11:33–36; MATTHEW 16:13–20

The Gospel we have just heard is one of the key passages in the Scriptures for the Catholic Church: It is the foundation for our doctrine and practices regarding the papacy. For this reason, it is also one of the most controversial passages. Try asking your fundamentalist friends why they don't read this passage literally, and note the far-fetched interpretations you get in response. Here are some examples:

> The passage that speaks of Peter as the rock upon which Jesus will build his church is not found in the other Gospels, so it must be something the Church added later on to justify the Roman Papacy.

> The rock to which Jesus refers is not really Peter but Peter's faith, so faith is the foundation of the Church.

> When Jesus said, "On this rock I will build my church," he was pointing to himself, because he is the stone rejected by the builders that has become the cornerstone.

Fortunately, advances in biblical scholarship and ecumenism have taken us beyond the old Catholic/Protestant arguments. Dr. Reginald Fuller, a highly respected Episcopalian biblical scholar, describes the current consensus on this passage as well as anyone I know. There are three points to be made: First, the scene is reconstructed by Matthew to reflect a post-resurrection setting. When we compare Matthew's material with Mark's, we see that Matthew added material: The confession of the divinity of Jesus and the conferring of authority on Peter would come from an encounter with the Risen Lord and post-resurrection faith. It would parallel chapter 21 in the Gospel of John, where the Risen Christ tells Peter to tend his flock and feed his sheep.

Second, there is general consensus that the rock on which Jesus wants to build his Church is Peter himself, not his faith or declaration of faith. Third, on the question of whether the role of Peter was to continue in the Christian community after his death, scholars are divided along denominational lines. Protestant scholars would say that Peter's role was foundational in the original community of disciples, but that then the power of binding and loosing passed to the church as a whole. Catholic scholars would argue that the need for Peter's role continues in the subsequent generations of disciples and is vested in the papacy.

Most Christian churches would agree and function out of the conviction that the people of God need to be organized and structured along the lines of human institutions. Some would even recognize the need for a central symbol of unity, for someone to represent and speak for the whole church. For better and for worse, Christianity has to deal with the fact of its institutional reality.

I say "for better *and* for worse" because while the institutional church has great accomplishments to its credit, it is also responsible for major problems and tragic mistakes. As long as we have an institution with humans in authority, we have to be prepared for human weakness and human perversion. In the first reading, God is ready to remove Shebna from office because he had made a mess of things. Unfortunately, his successor, Eliakim, did not turn out to be any better. Today's Gospel passage continues with Jesus' prediction of his passion and death, and his rebuke to Peter: "Get behind me, Satan! You are a stumbling block to me . . ." because Peter was trying to dissuade him from his mission. And if you know Church history, you know that among the popes we have both great saints and great sinners.

And yet the Church continues. In 1963, after the first session of the Second Vatican Council, Hugo Rahner, the brother of theologian Karl Rahner and a fine theologian in his own right, wrote an essay titled "The Church, God's Strength in Human Weakness"[41] that made a powerful impression on me. I have never forgotten it, and it has helped me immensely. He starts with Paul, who says: "If I must boast, I will boast of the things that concern my weakness" (2 Cor. 11:30) because, as he states, "the power of God reaches perfection in weakness" (2 Cor. 12:9). Hugo Rahner writes:

> Let us therefore attempt to see the mystery of the frail and wretched Church against the background of biblical theology and the history of her existence on earth up to now. Then this hour of celebration may become an hour of consolation, and the hard bread we must break may still satisfy us when the feast of lofty thoughts is over. Three fundamental notions should guide us in our quest: The Church of weakness is for us a fact of faith, a test of faith, and a joy of faith.[42]

That the Church of God here on earth "is always both strength and weakness, glory and wretchedness" is a fact of faith. We have to believe that God chooses to accomplish his purposes through weakness, if we believe that our salvation comes from the Eternal Word sharing our human flesh, dying the disgraceful human death on the cross. It is the seemingly powerless victim who says: "I have overcome the world" (John 16:33). The Church will continue to reflect all the weakness of which human beings are capable.

In addition to being a fact of faith, the Church of weakness is also a test of our faith, and sometimes even a danger to faith—a trying, discouraging, burning anxiety. Whenever we, the Church as a whole, or groups and individuals in the Church, fail to embody and express the saving love of God, we make it difficult for ourselves and for others to see that love at work in the world. We became a shame for faith. Augustine wrote:

> Those who were already standing near me ready to believe were frightened away by the life of wicked and false Christians. How many, my brothers, do you think would wish fervently to be Christians, but would be insulted by their terrible morals.[43]

But this weak Church is also the joy of our faith, when we put our trust in the victory of the Lord of the Church, Jesus Christ, when we humbly realize that, in the mystery of his wisdom and love, God has chosen to work with us and through us, with all our weaknesses and failures, to attain both the daily and final victories that will reveal his goodness and perfection. God's infinite power is made perfect through our weakness.

I have been reflecting a great deal on these ideas after reading the news stories about Archbishop Marino and the church in Atlanta; about Father Bruce Ritter, the founder of Covenant House; and about the new book by A.W. Richard Sipe, *A Secret World: Sexuality and the Search for Celibacy*. The Church's requirement of celibacy for all ordained clergy, except permanent deacons, is an area where the human weakness of many of the Church's ministers is becoming glaringly manifest. I would like to share my thoughts on this with you.

✢ I call on you to think of all who are touched by scandal with great compassion and sympathy. I call on you to continue to love this Church, in all its weakness, because it is still the body of Christ and the bride he has chosen for himself, even with all its unfaithfulness.

✢ I would call with passion on the pope and bishops of the Church, if only I could be heard, to study and discuss openly, honestly, with deep sensitivity and understanding, the question of mandatory celibacy for priests. It is a Church rule that needs to be seriously re-examined and perhaps changed. While freely chosen celibacy is a true gospel value and vocation, a powerful and necessary sign for the Church of our day, obligatory celibacy as now imposed seems to be doing great harm to the Church.

✢ I am completely convinced that, given the current law of the Church, if one chooses to continue to function as a priest in the Catholic Church one must remain faithful to the requirement of celibacy. Otherwise, the priest's life becomes a lie. I believe that if a priest finds celibacy no longer possible, if he finds it humanly destructive or no longer meaningful in his relationship with God, then he should leave the ranks of the clergy to avoid misrepresenting who he is and how he lives, to avoid becoming a scandal, an obstacle to faith.

I know no better way to conclude what I have been trying to say than to repeat Paul's conclusion to his long struggle with the question of the salvation of his own people. His words say to me that it is God's world, God's Church, God's salvation, and that we belong to God with all our weakness and whatever goodness we might be capable of through his power.

O the depth of the riches and wisdom and knowledge of God! How unsearchable are his judgments and how inscrutable his ways! 'For who has known the mind of the Lord? Or who has been his counselor? Or who has given a gift to him, to receive a gift in return?' For from him and through him and to him are all things. To him be the glory forever. Amen. (Rom. 11:33–36)

# Coming to Terms with the Cross

TIME: SEPTEMBER 2, 1984
SEASON: TWENTY-SECOND SUNDAY IN ORDINARY TIME
SCRIPTURE READINGS: JEREMIAH 20:7–9; ROMANS 12:1–2; MATTHEW 16:21–27

All human relationships have their good times and their bad times, moments of great joy and moments of unbearable pain. Try to remember a time in your own life when you quarreled and were angry with someone you loved; a time when you felt used or deceived by a friend; a time when you felt that another person had taken advantage of you, overwhelmed you through a power play or clever game-playing. That is the way Jeremiah felt!

In last Sunday's Gospel, Jesus blessed Peter and was ready to turn over to him the keys to his house and his project, the building of the kingdom of God. In today's reading, he calls him Satan, a devil, and chases him away, using the same words he had used against Satan in the story of his temptation in the desert! And this simply because Peter cares enough about Jesus not to want him to suffer and get himself killed. What is going on?

No personal relationship, not even a personal, loving relationship with God, is a guarantee of instant or constant happiness. People who tell you that if you are a Christian you should always be radiantly happy do not understand the full meaning of Christianity. People who tell you that if you have the Lord in your heart you will always have a smile on your face are telling you to be phony. Read today's passage from Jeremiah to those people. He feels that God has taken advantage of him. He accepted the prophetic call, he has been faithful and obedient to God, with the result that he has become an object of derision and mockery and rejection. Jeremiah wants to give up his prophetic speaking, but he can't do that because God will not let go of him.

Peter is well-intentioned and cares about Jesus, but he also completely misunderstands the meaning of Jesus' messiahship and of his own discipleship. He is also looking for the happy times and the glory days and the smiling faces. Peter really does not want to hear about Jesus suffering and dying, because he has a strong suspicion that the same fate is waiting for him. He is right. Jesus says: "If any want to become my followers, let them deny themselves and take up their cross and follow me. For those who want to save their life will lose it, and those who lose their life for my sake will find it. For what will it profit them if they gain the whole world but forfeit their life? Or what will they give in return for their life?"

Peter is human. Who wants to hear that kind of invitation and promise? Do you want to hear those words? I don't! But there they are, and they are addressed to us—if we want to follow Jesus, if we want to be his disciples!

The cross: We have made it into an ornament to wear around our necks; we have covered it with jewels and used silver and gold to make it precious and beautiful. We would rather forget that it was an instrument of torture and death, that it is a symbol of saving, redemptive suffering and dying.

The cross is the inseparable companion of anyone who wants to follow Jesus. And it is not his cross that we are asked to carry, but ours. What is our cross? What is your cross today?

Not many of us are going to be put in prison or thrown to the bottom of a dry well because of our prophetic activities as Jeremiah was. Not many of us are going to be actually nailed to a cross as Peter was. But all of us are asked to take up our cross. It is our choice. Jesus is not talking about the burden of the cross falling on us and crushing us. We have to take it willingly. This is the sign of discipleship. What are we asked to do?

Perhaps the brief passage from Paul offers us a clue: Do not conform yourselves to this age! Do not just go along with the crowd. Do not accept uncritically the values of your culture, of your world, of your peers, of the media, of the opinion-makers and the creators of fads. That is something we can choose to do or not to do, and how difficult it is to be different, to march to a different drummer.

A psychiatrist has described what he calls "the American Fairy Tale." He suggests that it has five main theses:

> 1. *More possessions mean more happiness in life.* You could have fooled me! I am still hoping to win the lottery!

> 2. *A person who does more or produces more is better and more important.* The Associated Press recently reported the story of a teenager named Amy. She was 15, a straight-A student, and was very upset because she got a B. Her parents were even more upset. She wrote them a note: "If I fail in what I do, I fail in what I am." After writing the note, she committed suicide.

> 3. *Everyone must identify with and belong to a larger group in life.* Happiness, well-being, success require that we belong to the majority.

> 4. *Perfect mental health means having no problems in life.* The only real problems are the ones we create ourselves. To put it another way, positive thinking conquers everything.

> 5. *A person is abnormal unless he or she is constantly happy with life.* You are not a good Christian if you are not always happy and smiling.

If the psychiatrist is correct in his description of our cultural values, then Paul tells us: Do not be like that!

The invitation today is to consider carefully the consequences of being a disciple of Jesus in our time, and to ask ourselves: Do I really want to follow Jesus? Do I really want to take up my cross, whatever it may turn out to be? What will happen to me if I say "yes"?

People who are open to getting behind Jesus and following him must be ready for Calvary as well as the empty tomb, for Good Friday as well as for Easter. The disciple must be ready every day to participate in the paschal mystery of Jesus, in his death and in his resurrection. As in all personal, loving relationships, when the going gets difficult, the question is: Is it worth it? Do I love the Lord enough to follow him?

# Says Who?

TIME: SEPTEMBER 6, 1987
SEASON: TWENTY-THIRD SUNDAY IN ORDINARY TIME
SCRIPTURE READINGS: EZEKIEL 33:7–9; ROMANS 13:8–10; MATTHEW 18:15–20

Watchmen served an important function in ancient Israel. During harvest time, men were hired to protect the crops against thieves, and often a stone tower was erected in the fields to provide a vantage point for keeping an eye on the surrounding countryside. In the cities, sentinels stood guard in the towers of the city walls and cried out the alarm if an enemy was seen approaching.

Ezekiel, like the other prophets, describes himself as the watchman of the house of Israel. The message he proclaims is the warning that comes from God. Ezekiel is speaking to people suffering the pain of defeat and exile, people who keep blaming their forebears for the judgment that the present generation is forced to bear, thus calling God's justice into question. Ezekiel warns them of their personal responsibility, and calls them to repentance.

There are many people today who see the pope and bishops and Roman congregations as the watchmen of the Church who should warn the faithful and the world of their wicked ways. They would like to see the Church run like a tight ship, where discipline is strictly enforced and everything is done by the book. They appeal to passages like the Gospel reading we heard two weeks ago, where Peter was given the power to bind and to loose, and the Gospel passage we heard today, which speaks of excommunicating people if they ignore the Church: Gentiles and tax collectors were excluded from the synagogue. But is that really the best way to exercise authority in the Church?

To begin our reflection on this question, please note that Ezekiel, once he has proclaimed his warning, has fulfilled his responsibility. Now the listener must decide what to do. And note that in this Gospel passage the authority to bind and loose is given to the whole community of disciples. In the passage from Romans, Paul tells us that the only debt we owe one another is to love one another.

In the Church there will always be tension between the exercise of authority, which is absolutely necessary, and the exercise of freedom, which is also essential. Things have changed dramatically in the past thirty to forty years. The range of freedom, not only in the Church but in society as a whole, has steadily increased. More and more people are capable of learning, of reflecting on their experience, of questioning and thinking for themselves. The ideal would be to be able to resolve all conflicts through dialogue in order to reach a free, informed assent. I believe that is the way God works with us, moving us by gentle persuasion, patiently meeting us where we are and urging us, empowering us, to grow.

An interviewer once asked the theologian Karl Rahner if there are times when Catholics could freely disagree with the pope. He answered: "Of course." He gave some examples, such as the question of whether or not the pope should receive controversial political figures (such as Yasar Arafat or Kurt Waldheim), or whether the pope should recognize the state of Israel and give up the Vatican position of the internationalization of Jerusalem. These are certainly issues on which Catholics, even bishops and cardinals, disagree.

In discussing the possibility of disagreement in other areas, Rahner stated that "truth is a rather complicated matter." He gave an example that may help all of us who wrestle with the tension of authority and freedom. A physician gives his best-informed opinion that a patient should undergo an operation. The patient acts upon it. But the physician may be wrong, and research even then under way may before long provide a better, more correct diagnosis. That does not mean that the patient should have ignored the advice of the physician. But it does mean that the patient should be free to go against that advice or seek a second opinion.

Returning to the discussion of theology, Rahner gave the example of the question of the authorship of the Pentateuch, the first five books of the Hebrew Scriptures, which were

decreed by Pope Pius X to have been written by Moses. In 1910 Father Henry Poels was dismissed from his teaching position at the Catholic University of America for refusing to sign an oath stating that in conscience he believed the contents of that decision. The Church now recognizes that Pius X was incorrect. Scholarship has produced a new answer, just as medical research produces new answers.

Rahner gave a more whimsical example of authority reversing itself, telling of a meeting with Pope Paul VI. Rahner said to the pope: "At one time I was forbidden to write anything more about concelebration. Now you yourself concelebrate." The pope answered a bit enigmatically, with a smile: "Yes, there is a time for laughing, and a time for crying."[44]

Do you agree with the official teaching of the Church on abortion, birth control, divorce, premarital sex, homosexuality, married priests, women priests? If you disagree, have you prayed and agonized over your conclusion and decision? Have you thoroughly investigated and discussed and reflected? Do you hold your opinion with humility and a certain sadness, because you have the highest respect for the authority of the pope and bishops in the Church, and you are uncomfortable with a position of disagreement and dissent?

That is the way I feel, the way I approach my own struggle with questions of authority in teachings and discipline in the Church. I agree with Karl Rahner, as I quoted him today. I am absolutely committed to the ancient formula that has been repeated so many times through the centuries about this issue: "In all necessary, essential matters there should be unity, in doubtful matters freedom, in all things charity, love."

# Our Need to Forgive

TIME: SEPTEMBER 15, 1996
SEASON: TWENTY-FOURTH SUNDAY IN ORDINARY TIME
SCRIPTURE READINGS: SIRACH 27:30–28:7; ROMANS 14:7–9; MATTHEW 18:21–35

I would like to share with you a contemporary story of forgiveness that comes to us from Galilee. But before I do that, I want to mention a story I saw on the NBC news last evening. I wish I had all the details to tell you the full story. Some thirty or so years ago a ten-year-old boy was kidnapped, tortured, shot in the head and left for dead. Miraculously, he survived, losing his left eye and suffering some other minor impairments. The kidnapper was never found, but recently he confessed to the crime. He is an old man, confined to bed in a nursing home. The boy, now a grown man, of course, has gone to visit his kidnapper to offer his forgiveness and to reassure him of God's forgiveness. The news clip showed the two men praying together. That is what the gospel is all about.

I found the other story in a magazine called *Living Prayer*.[45] Galilee is the area where Jesus was when he told the parable we heard in today's Gospel passage. In northern Galilee there is an ancient village on a hilltop, surrounded by olive trees, called Ibillin. The village has a regional high school, a community center, and a library, where there is a beautiful sign in Arabic that reads:

> God is the creator of all human beings, with their differences, their colors, their races, their religions. Be attentive: Every time you draw nearer to your neighbor, your draw nearer to God. Be attentive: Every time you go further from your neighbor, you go further from God.

Many of the good things that have happened in the village have been attributed to Father Elias Chacour, a Melkite priest who is the pastor in the village. When he arrived in Ibillin many years ago, the church was falling down and the congregation that gathered there was divided. When the people came to church they clustered in four separate groups, keeping distance from each other, looking at each other with grim faces. The root of the division was the enmity between four brothers, who had refused to be together in the same room even when their mother died. During Fr. Elias's first year as pastor, on Palm Sunday, he looked out at the stony faces before him. One of the brothers sat in the first row with his wife and children. Hymns were sung, but without any spirit. Readings were proclaimed, the sermon was preached, but there was no life. Fr. Elias recalls: "The congregation endured me indifferently, fulfilling their Sunday obligation to warm the benches."

Before the service ended that day, Fr. Elias did something that took everyone by surprise, including himself. He walked to the back of the church and padlocked the door. Returning to the front of the church, he told the parishioners:

> Sitting in this building does not make you a Christian. You are a people divided. If you can't love your brother whom you see, how can you say that you love God who is invisible? You have allowed the Body of Christ to be disgraced. I have tried for months to unite you. I have failed. I am only a man. But there is someone else who can bring you together in true unity. His name is Jesus Christ. He has the power to forgive you. So now I will be quiet and allow him to give you that power. If you will not forgive, then we stay locked in here. If you want, you can kill each other, and I'll provide your funeral free.

Ten minutes passed, but for Fr. Elias it seemed like eternity. Then the policeman stood up, faced the congregation, bowed his head and said: "I am sorry. I am the worst of all. I have hated my own brothers. I have hated them so much that I wanted to kill them. More than any of you I need forgiveness." He turned to Fr. Elias: "Father, can you forgive me?" "Come here," Fr. Elias replied. They embraced each other with the kiss of peace. "Now go and greet your brothers." The four brothers rushed together, meeting halfway down the aisle, and in tears forgave each other. "In an instant," Fr. Elias recalls, "the church was a chaos of embracing and repentance." Fr. Elias had to shout to make his next words audible: "Dear friends, we are not going to wait until next week to celebrate the Resurrection. Let us begin now. We were dead to each other. Now we are alive again." He began to sing: "Christ is risen from the dead. By his death he has trampled death and given life to those in the tomb." The congregation joined the hymn. Unchaining the door, Fr. Elias led them into the streets.

"For the rest of the day and far into the evening," he continues, "I joined groups of believers as they went from house to house. At every door, someone had to ask forgiveness for some wrong. Never was forgiveness withheld." Now, in this village in northern Israel, Palestinians, both Christian and Muslim, work together to build a community.

The people in that church learned well the lesson that both the first reading from the Hebrew Scriptures and the reading from the Gospel of Matthew are trying to teach us today. God's people must be a forgiving people, because our God is a God whose forgiveness is without limits. The voice of the great teacher speaks to us from the second century before Christ:

> Forgive your neighbor's injustice;
> then when you pray, your own sins will be forgiven.
> Does anyone harbor anger against another,
> and expect healing from the Lord?
> If we have no mercy toward one another
> can we then seek pardon for our own sins? (Sir. 28:3–5)

Jesus proclaims to us the same message in the Gospel: "My heavenly Father will treat you exactly the same way unless each of you forgives one another from the heart" (Matt. 18:35).

There is a passage in the Gospels that speaks of the unforgivable sin, the sin against the Holy Spirit, but we really do not know what that means. I don't know of any other circumstances in which the Scriptures suggest that God might not give his forgiveness, except when we fail to forgive one another. The whole of chapter 18 of the Gospel of Matthew has to do with the community of disciples, how to handle problems, the need for discipline in the community, how leaders should behave, and the parable of the unforgiving servant we heard today. Mutual forgiveness and reconciliation are absolutely crucial in any community. The inability to forgive, holding onto grudges, seeking vengeance, are the most destructive forces in a community, whether it be a family, the extended family, a work situation, a church community, a civil community, a nation.

Our civil society and our American Church are among the most diverse kinds of communities in the world. There are more differences, and more profound differences, among us because of color, race, religion, ethnicity, gender, sexual orientation, life styles, than in perhaps any other country in the world. There are some who would like to exploit these differences among us for personal gain, for political reasons, people who would set one group against another and exploit the fears, the misconceptions, the misinformation that all of us have, in ways that would further divide us and threaten even more our fragile communities. I believe that as Christians, as disciples of the Jesus who came to reveal God's mercy and love, God's compassion and forgiveness that embrace the whole human family, we are called to resist these efforts to divide us and exacerbate the hurts and hatreds and fears that already exist among us.

As always, I believe, we must begin with ourselves and our own situations. We need to ask ourselves: Is there someone against whom I hold resentment and hatred, someone whom I have not been able to forgive? Is there someone who needs and waits for my forgiveness for what he or she has done to me? Is there someone from whom I need to beg forgiveness for the wrong that I have done to him or her? There is no mistaking the call, the challenge of today's biblical readings: We must forgive one another, we must seek and become the instruments of reconciliation.

Perhaps we are afraid that we cannot do it, that we cannot let go of our wounds and our anger, our pride and self-righteousness. We are correct. By ourselves we cannot do it. But there is someone here among us who has the power to forgive us and who empowers us to forgive. His name is Jesus Christ. It is the same Jesus who motivated the young man to forgive his kidnapper, who transformed the people in that church in the village in Galilee into a people of reconciliation, a Christian community of love and forgiveness. He can do it again, he can do it for each of us, if we let him.

## It's Not Fair!

TIME: SEPTEMBER 23, 1990
SEASON: TWENTY-FIFTH SUNDAY IN ORDINARY TIME
SCRIPTURE READINGS: ISAIAH 55:6–9;
    PHILIPPIANS 1:20C–24, 27A; MATTHEW 20:1–16A

One of the most effective ways of using the Bible for your prayer and reflection, for the nurturing and deepening of your relationship with God, is to put yourself in the scene described by a particular passage and to identify yourself as one of the characters of the story. In the chapter of Matthew that precedes today's reading, we find the story of the rich young man who comes to Jesus seeking something more than obedience to the law, and who leaves in sadness because he can't let go of his possessions in order to follow Jesus. Jesus comments on how hard it is for the rich to enter the kingdom of heaven.[46]

Peter insists: What about us? We left everything to follow you! What are we going to get? And Jesus answers: You will receive a hundredfold and inherit eternal life. But he immediately adds: "But many who are first will be last, and the last will be first." In today's parable of the laborers in the vineyard, Matthew has Jesus say again that "the last will be first, and the first will be last."

In today's parable the owner of the vineyard obviously is God, as we are told in the first verse that the kingdom of God is like this story. In the story the owner goes out to hire workers for his vineyard at dawn, at ten in the morning, at noon, at three in the afternoon, and at five in the afternoon. When darkness comes, the workers gather to receive their pay. The first ones hired have worked ten to twelve hours; the last hired have worked two hours at most, but all workers receive the same pay. Those who have worked hard all day complain, and the owner replies: Where is the injustice? I gave you the agreed-upon and standard wage for a day's work. Why can't I be generous to the others with my money, if I want to?

Did you identify with a particular group of workers? Where did you see yourself in that line moving slowly toward the foreman who is passing out the money? I suspect that most of us would see ourselves at the end of the line, with the workers who were hired first. Most of us work hard; we try to be good; we come to church; we make sacrifices for our children, for our parish community; we help the poor when we can; we pray and are faithful to God.

I certainly see myself in that group. I was baptized two weeks after I was born; I studied for twelve years to become a priest; I left my family, my friends, my country to come serve the Lord here in the Central Valley because I was told that there was a great need for priests here. I have done everything that I was asked to do. I feel that I try to do the best I can, and I spend myself in faithful ministry. And now I hear Jesus say that all that does not make any difference, that I am going to be last, that some lazy scoundrel who has hardly contributed anything for the kingdom of God will get the same reward! I am not a happy camper!

I was trying to rewrite the parable in modern terms, and I thought of a couple of ways to do so. Imagine yourself having died and gone to heaven. After the initial joy of being there, meeting God face to face, greeting all the people you loved, you start looking around. At first you can't believe your eyes, but you look again and you ask around and yes, that is really Saddam Hussein, and there is that vicious murderer who so richly deserved the death penalty, and there is that drug pusher who got one of your children hooked, and the spouse who abused you and your children and made life impossible for you, and your boss who humiliated you and harassed you and drove you out of your mind, and there are those burglars who broke into your house and took all the things that had so much sentimental value for you. What's going on here? How did they get here? And how does God answer your complaint? "My ways are not your ways; my thoughts are not your thoughts. I am generous in forgiving all who turn to me for mercy, no matter when they do it. Are you envious because I am generous?"

Another way that occurred to me of redoing the parable in modern form is less dramatic but more concrete for my own personal experience. At one time I had some idea about teaching full-time at the university. I soon realized that it could never happen. The department of my specialty was all white and all male, and many women and individuals from minority groups with good qualifications were applying for the same positions. They would be hired, and I would not. Those who at one time were hired last or not hired at all because of discriminatory practices now are hired first.

What does all this mean? That it does not matter what I do or how I live? Of course not. That the better way is to sit around and enjoy myself, do what I please, look out for myself and get all I can get of this world's goods and pleasures, and wait for that last call to work in the Lord's vineyard, when I am old and it's time to settle accounts? I don't think so. I will tell you the lessons I learned from today's texts.

First, I want to learn to be as generous as God is, as generous to others as God is to me. I want the goodness of the Lord to be revealed in the salvation of all, especially those who seem most closely allied with the powers of evil, because then the victory of God's goodness will be all the greater. I want to be able to affirm with inexpressible joy the freedom of God to do what he pleases with his money, to lavish his love generously on everyone, even those who resist that love to the very end and fight him to their last breath.

Second, I want to learn that God's call to me to work in his vineyard from early morning until darkness is not a burden but a privilege. It is a gift, the most wonderful, generous, loving gift that God can give to anyone, to be called to be a worker in his kingdom side by side with his beloved Son, to help build a new earth where the goodness of God will reign and all evil will be conquered, even death.

One day this week I started with a meeting at 7 a.m., worked through lunch, skipped dinner because I had no time to eat, and got home at 9:30 p.m.—fourteen and a half hours of work without a break. I was feeling sorry for myself until I started working on the biblical texts for today, and then I was glad that, by the grace of God, I was able to give a full day in his service. And I was filled with joy and gratitude and new energy. It is grace, amazing grace, that God would choose to work the creative transformation of his kingdom through our feeble forces and our sinful weakness.

I hope you will share this response to the Gospel message, that you will try to match God's generosity to you, that you will be able to rejoice in God's call to serve him at this moment, at this stage of your life journey, as your parish community calls you to faithful stewardship of the gifts that God has given you, to faithful service in his kingdom with all your energy and talents. Try to match God's generosity to you, and see what happens!

## Big Talk, No Do

TIME: SEPTEMBER 28, 1975
SEASON: TWENTY-SIXTH SUNDAY IN ORDINARY TIME
SCRIPTURE READINGS: EZEKIEL 18:25–28; PHILIPPIANS 2:1–11; MATTHEW 21:28–32

Being a Christian person or a Christian community involves more than just feelings or beautiful words. Today's readings seem to say to us: "Put your actions where your words are. Change your way of life in accordance with your faith." Once again we are called to confront the paradox of our own life with the discrepancy between our words and our actions, our ideals and the reality of our daily life.

A great deal of tension comes through in the Gospel story we heard today. The setting itself is one of conflict and antagonism and controversy. Jesus has just come into Jerusalem, and Matthew has just described the incident of Jesus becoming angry in the temple and driving away the buyers and the sellers, the act that led the leaders of the people, whom Matthew identifies as the chief priests and the elders, to come and question Jesus: "By what authority are you doing these things, and who gave you this authority?" (Matt. 21:23b) The series of confrontations that follow, like the one described today, build up in a continuing crescendo to the betrayal and capture, the trial and death of Jesus.

Of course, today's story is really told to put the leaders on the spot. Jesus asks them to commit themselves, and the way in which they commit themselves will convict them. "What do you think of this case?" he asks them. "Which of the two sons did what is right?" The answer is obvious: The son who repents of his refusal and goes to work is the one who does the will of the father. The point Matthew wanted to make in using this story is clear. He is writing to a Jewish audience, and he is saying to them: "You are the yes-man, the son who said he would go to work but did not do so, because you accepted the covenant, you have been calling yourselves God's special people, but you have not followed through. You haven't kept your part of the covenant. And now the people on whom you have looked as being sinners—the tax collectors and prostitutes, will enter the kingdom of heaven ahead of you because they have repented. They have believed in the preaching of John. They have changed their lives."

The Gospel has some echoes of that first reading from Ezekiel, which doesn't seem to make much sense unless you see it in context. The context is a major turning point in the development of Old Testament thought. Up to this point, the punishment for sin was seen as a collective thing where the whole people was involved. Now, the emphasis is on personal responsibility. God is no longer going to punish the sins of the fathers in their children and grandchildren to the third and fourth generation. Each one is now responsible for his own life. And in the parable of the two sons we are being told that it is not enough to say: "We are the children of Abraham, followers of Moses. We obey the law. We fast on fast days. We say our prayers. We pay our tithes. And therefore we are the children of the Father." It is not enough anymore.

And now, before we allow ourselves almost unconsciously to slip into even the mildest form of anti-Semitism, letting our feelings go in the direction of saying: "How blind and how stubborn were those Jewish leaders who couldn't understand that parable and kept fighting with Jesus," we ought to look very carefully at ourselves, because we may find ourselves in exactly the same position. For it is not enough to say: "I am a Christian; I am a disciple of Jesus Christ; and I proclaim, as Paul tells me to do, Jesus Christ is Lord." That is not sufficient for the assurance of salvation and the guarantee of righteousness. It is not enough for us to say, "I go to Mass every Sunday, and I support the Church, and I obey the commandments." That's not enough either.

Today's texts and liturgy are a warning to us that we must not look at ourselves smugly as children of God and heirs of his promises and the gathering of his kingdom simply because we call ourselves Christian or Catholic and a Christian community. We ought to look around to see what other people are doing. And we might discover that there are those who, without any explicit profession of faith in Jesus Christ, are going about doing the works of his kingdom which perhaps we are not doing, the works of the kingdom as proclaimed in Isaiah and appropriated by Jesus in his own preaching. They are going about proclaiming and giving hope to the poor and the downtrodden, feeding the hungry, giving freedom to the oppressed, healing the sick, giving sight to the blind. And those are the ones who are entering the kingdom of God ahead of us, unless we also repent and live out our faith in the midst of the practical realities of our daily life.

The Gospel story does not have a third son, one who willingly and joyfully says to the father, "Yes, I will go," and then actually goes to do the work that has been given to him. But the second reading describes such a son in a magnificent statement that is probably one of the very ancient Christian hymns that Paul incorporated into his own letters. In that hymn, Jesus is described as one who is not afraid to let go of his exalted position and assume a human life and a human existence, with all that involves, for the sake of others. He is described as the one who not only becomes man but becomes obedient unto death, even death on the cross.

It is in him, then, that the inconsistency between saying and doing, which is exemplified in the two sons in the Gospel story, is finally overcome—in Jesus, the son of God. His "yes" carries him even to the point of becoming obedient unto death. And Paul says to the Christians of Philippi: "Your attitude must be Christ's attitude," the attitude described in that ancient hymn. And then Paul makes some specific applications for the Christians to whom he is writing. He says in a slightly different translation from the one we heard: "There must be no competition among you, no conceit. Everyone is to be self-effacing. Always consider the other person to be better than yourselves so that nobody thinks of his own interest first, but everybody thinks of other people's interests, instead."

I don't think there is any question about the fact that Paul's instruction is given to us also. He is saying to us, even today: "Your attitude must be Christ's attitude."

# Laboring in the Vineyard

TIME: OCTOBER 4, 1987
SEASON: TWENTY-SEVENTH SUNDAY IN ORDINARY TIME
SCRIPTURE READINGS: ISAIAH 5:1–7; PHILIPPIANS 4:6–9; MATTHEW 21:33–43

For the past three Sundays the Gospel readings have presented to us images of vineyards. First we heard about workers called to the vineyard at the different hours of the day but all receiving the same wage. Then we heard about the reactions of two sons sent by their father to work in the vineyard. Today we hear about tenants who rebel and others who are entrusted with the vineyard.

It is a good time for us to reflect on vineyards, and about work in the vineyard, and about harvests. These images are not foreign to us: We are surrounded by recently harvested vineyards; we read a lot about workers in the vineyards. Let the images of our rich valley make very concrete the sayings of Jesus and the lessons of the Gospels.

The first reading gives us the background and the key to understanding the Gospel. It is one of the most beautiful and dramatic poems in the prophetic literature. Imagine this scene: It is a harvest festival and the prophet begins by singing a song about a splendid vineyard belonging to a friend. But the song ends with a sour note, because the vineyard bears no good grapes.

The scene shifts to a courtroom, and the friend calls upon the people to adjudicate the dispute between himself and his vineyard, and the judgment is against the vineyard. And then comes the punch line: The friend is God, and the vineyard is the house of Israel, and the complaint is that they have produced only bloodshed and injustice, and the cries of the poor and the oppressed rise up to God.

In the Gospel it is still the same vineyard, but now it takes on a new dimension: It has become the kingdom of God, and Jesus sees himself as the special son of the Father, the last of the messengers to be sent, facing death as his destiny, raising the question: To whom will the kingdom of God be entrusted?

In the Gospel of Matthew, the Church is entrusted with the responsibility for the kingdom, and by this time the Gentiles were taking over. It would be easy to turn this parable into one more tale of "how the Jews missed the boat," but if we did that we would miss the impact of the parable, which is directed to whomever has the care of the vineyard. If we think that God has entrusted his kingdom to us, then the parable is directed to us: Do we bring forth good fruit, do we yield a rich harvest? If we don't, it will be taken away from us. It is being said more and more frequently that in the twenty-first century the first world, the Western world, will be evangelized by the Third World, because the Christians in the Third World have a more vital faith, and because they are more willing servants.

All the parables of the vineyard are stories of disappointed expectations. What are we called upon to do in our time? Not to convert the world to Christ in one generation; we have been trying for three generations and more and we have not succeeded. Not to establish one triumphal church everywhere; it seems increasingly clear that true Christianity will always be a minority religion. We are called upon to live the gospel and by our life to make Christ present everywhere. This will happen only through the witness of our life, a life dedicated to making gentle the way of the world, to taming the angry lion still roaring within us, to becoming more human, as Jesus was human. It will happen if we promote life and not bloodshed, justice rather than injustice, and if we hear the cry of the poor and the oppressed.

Today we are invited to observe "Respect Life" Sunday. I like very much the image proposed by Cardinal Bernardin of Chicago, who speaks of life as a "seamless robe." Our commitment to life must include all of life, from the womb to the tomb, for rich and poor nations, whether life be threatened by abortion on demand or by starvation, by violence in war or in the home, by communism or consumerism, by guns or by drugs. Our commitment must be to life with dignity for everyone and for the survival of our planet.

What are the fruits of my life? What have I done that I would like to leave behind, besides unanswered letters, unpaid charge accounts, and a lot of toys? We are responsible to God for our work in his vineyard, for the shape we give our life, for the way we love or fail to love, for the way we make money, for the way we relate to one another and participate in the life of the various communities to which we belong, for the way we use our talents or neglect them.

But no matter what our failings may be we remain the cherished plants, the carefully tended vineyard of the Lord's own cultivation. The prophet is speaking of God as a friend. This is the marvel and the mystery of our relationship with God. Even if we fail him, he will not fail us. He may complain and be angry with us, he may let us face the consequences of our mistakes and failures, but he will not abandon us. He has not abandoned the Jews; they are still his cherished plant: We have Paul's word for this. And he remains present to us as every form of love we have experienced: father, mother, lover, spouse, host, companion, friend. May his peace, which surpasses all understanding, continue to guard our minds and our hearts in Christ Jesus. And may the sacrament of his death and resurrection help us to meet the challenge of his word.

## RSVP: Come to the Banquet

TIME: OCTOBER 13, 1996
SEASON: TWENTY-EIGHTH SUNDAY IN ORDINARY TIME
SCRIPTURE READINGS: ISAIAH 25:6–10A;
  PHILIPPIANS 4:12–14, 19–20; MATTHEW 22:1–14

We know that the evangelists, the Gospel writers, adapted the original parables of Jesus to fit their own historical situation and theological vision. By comparing different versions of the same parable in different Gospels and identifying the unique features of a particular evangelist, we are able to better understand what the writer is trying to say. Matthew's version of the parable of the great feast, which we heard today, has several unique features. In Matthew it is a king who is giving the feast, and the feast is for the wedding of his son. The guests receive two invitations to the feast. Not only is the second invitation rejected by the pre-invited guests, but they also treat the king's messengers violently—even killing some of them. The king responds in anger and destroys their city. When the servants go out into the street to gather in new guests, Matthew tells us that they bring in the bad as well as the good. Finally, Matthew gives us the strange incident of the guest just brought in from the street who is condemned because he is not properly dressed.

What is Matthew doing? He has turned the parable into two allegories to address the historical situation of Judaism and the early Christian community. The first allegory is about the history of Israel, as interpreted by Matthew. Israel ignored and mistreated the prophets, they rejected the son, and, by the time the Gospel of Matthew was written, they had suffered the destruction of the city and temple of Jerusalem, in the year 70 C.E. The second allegory is about the church, the community of believers who gave us the Gospel of Matthew, and who were discovering the fact that there were bad persons in the community as well as good persons. The guest without the wedding garment is someone within the church who has the wrong attitude, the wrong disposition, who has joined the church for the wrong reasons.

Just as Matthew adapted the parable to make a statement, to bring out the lesson for his own time, we need to hear the Gospel and the other Scripture readings for our own time and situation. What do these texts say to us today? What do they teach us?

My hearing of these texts reflects what happened to me this past week, during our annual clergy retreat. The retreat master, Fr. Martin Palmer, a Jesuit from St. Louis University, caught me completely by surprise and startled everyone. In his opening conference he stated that Catholics in growing numbers are leaving the Catholic Church and joining evangelical churches because they have not heard the gospel preached in the Catholic Church. I have been preaching for forty-three years: Have I failed to preach the gospel?

Fr. Palmer's point is that we preach the Church, the sacraments, morality, social consciousness, but we fail to preach Jesus Christ as the saving deed of God for our sinful world. The Christian gospel, the Good News that we are called to preach and to live, is that "God so loved the world that he gave his only Son, so that everyone who believes in him may not perish but may have eternal life" (John 3:16).

From the perspective of God, our world is a sinful world, alienated from God, either ignoring or rebelling against God. It is not just a matter of some people being good and others being bad, or some people being better and others being worse. It is the radical inability of humanity to enter into the right relationship with God by our own efforts. By ourselves we are unable to love God with our whole heart and mind and being, and to love our neighbor as we love ourselves. In answer to our radical sinfulness God sent his Son, "born of a woman, born under the law," to take upon himself our sinfulness, to die for our sins. "God proves his love of us in that while we were still sinners Christ died for us" (Rom. 5:8). God raised Jesus from the dead, and we are called to share in Christ's death and resurrection, in his victory over the powers of sin and death. The Christian Scriptures are full of different expressions of this Good News, of the heart of the gospel. Here is just one, from Paul's Letter to the Romans (3:22–25):

[T]here is no distinction, since [we] all have sinned and fall short of the glory of God; [we] are now justified by his grace as a gift, through the redemption that is in Christ Jesus, whom God put forward as a sacrifice of atonement by his blood, effective through faith.

All of us have sinned. All of us, by ourselves, left to our own resources, will always fail to be the kind of person or community that brings glory to God. We cannot save ourselves, no matter how hard we try. Our only possibility of salvation is to accept what God has done in Jesus Christ as a gift, to accept the gift in faith, faith expressing itself in love, love of God above all others, and love of neighbor in God.

If Fr. Palmer is right and this is the gospel we must preach with new urgency in our time, what is the message of today's Scripture readings? The texts are a powerful invitation to accept God's mystery of salvation in Jesus Christ in faith, without excuses, without running away from it, without letting the attractions and distractions of our sinful world become obstacles to our acceptance in faith.

At our retreat, I felt a strong and deep resistance to hearing and embracing the gospel from this radical perspective, but the more I thought about it, reflected on it, prayed about it, and let the gift and grace of God take over in me, the more I had to agree that there is no other way, no other answer, no other gospel. What about you? Do you also feel resistance to the gospel of Jesus Christ proclaimed in these terms? Do you find yourself looking for excuses right now to avoid answering the invitation to recognize our profound sinfulness and to accept the gift of salvation that God is offering us in his beloved Son?

It is God's gift, God's grace that brings us here together as a community of faith to celebrate the memory and the promise of the saving death and resurrection of Jesus. Our Eucharist here today is the anticipation and pledge of the wedding feast God has prepared for his Son. We have answered God's invitation, we have gathered for the feast. Do we have the wedding garment? Do we have the proper attitude, do we have the right disposition? That disposition means accepting our utter powerlessness before God, our sinful condition, and our desperate need for the gift of God's salvation in Jesus Christ. The right disposition for God's wedding feast is the acceptance in faith of the saving power of God in Christ Jesus. We still have Church and sacraments, moral conduct and integrity of life, concerns for justice and working for the coming of God's reign in our world. But we can only do all that in Christ and with Christ. As Paul said in the second reading: "In him who is the source of my strength I have strength for everything" (Phil 4:13).

Matthew's reading of the parable as a reference to the great messianic feast is right in line with the tradition of Isaiah as we heard it in the first reading, which tells us of the feast of God's salvation. Listen again. When that day comes we will be able to say: "Behold our God, to whom we looked to save us! This is the Lord to whom we looked; let us rejoice and be glad that he has saved us!" (Is. 25:10)

If he were writing today, perhaps Matthew would have used T. S. Eliot's play *The Cocktail Party* to illustrate the parable. Even if he would not have done it, I will:

> Guests at a cocktail party stand in small groups, as though ready to depart at a moment's notice, never seated together at a table. In Eliot's play the guests arrive, then depart abruptly; the cast of characters shifts about in continual coming and going. The Guardians, heavenly characters who attempt to guide the meaningless action toward transformation, repeatedly attempt to prepare a meal in the hosts' kitchen but are foiled by the lack of supplies and the lack of interest on the part of the guests. The larder is bare; the hearts of the hosts and guests are bare.[47]

Neither the great passage from Isaiah nor the beautiful Psalm 23 suggest that what God is preparing for us is a cocktail party! God prepares a sumptuous table for us, invites us to sit down and, in his love for us, shares the feast with us. It is a feast of rich, juicy food and pure, choice wine. It is the feast of God's beloved Son who died for our sins and was raised from the dead for our salvation. And everyone is invited!

## Overcoming Individualism

TIME: OCTOBER 18, 1987
SEASON: TWENTY-NINTH SUNDAY IN ORDINARY TIME
SCRIPTURE READINGS: ISAIAH 45:1, 4–6;
  1 THESSALONIANS 1:1–5B; MATTHEW 22:15–21

I am sorry to disappoint you, but Jesus says that we have to pay taxes! Perhaps the question of paying taxes is not as emotionally charged for us as it was in the days of Jesus. For him it was really a loaded question, asked to back him into a corner so that he would create more enemies for himself, no matter what he answered.

The Jews in Jesus' time were burdened by a double taxation: the "temple tax" to Jewish authorities and the tribute for the foreign power, Rome, that had conquered them. Rome collected its taxes on lands, harbors, and imports. Herod the Great imposed taxes on agriculture and on every piece of merchandise that was bought or sold. In addition, assessments were due on property, and customs duties were collected, not only at seaports but also at the gates of cities.

The coins of Jesus' day usually carried a figure of the emperor, often with a title implying his divinity, a further affront to the sensitivity of the Jews with their strict monotheism and proscription against making graven images of gods. We may complain about the amount we have to pay in taxes and about how our government spends our money, but at least these decisions are made by our elected representatives to whom we can express our opinions.

Aside from taxes, at times we use the phrase "give to Caesar what is Caesar's, but give to God what is God's" to justify our nation's constitutional separation of church and state, while at other times we identify Caesar with God and imply that disagreement with government policy is disloyalty to God.

I would like us to read and hear these words in the light of what I was trying to say last week about the need for a deeper consciousness of the fact that we are one world, one human family, with responsibilities that arise from the reality of our original and essential interconnectedness with everything and everyone. The book *Habits of the Heart* by Robert N. Bellah and his colleagues, from which I have quoted several times, is on its way to becoming an American classic. It is a sociological study of middle- to upper-middle-class America that reveals an almost exclusive preoccupation with "utilitarian individualism" and "expressive individualism."

By "utilitarian individualism" the authors mean a definition of personal identity based on economic and social status, and a form of social life that places minimal restraints on the individual pursuit of money, goods, and power. By "expressive individualism" they mean the search for meaning in individual expressions of feelings, in getting in touch with the deeper core of an inner self, with relationships based mostly on the therapeutic model of non-judgmental acceptance and support of each person.

The authors find these two forms of individualism in tension with the biblical ideal that promotes both a high respect for the dignity of each person and a sense of communal being, as God's people, in which we share a common destiny and a common responsibility. Individual and expressive utilitarianism are also in tension with the ideal of a "republican civic commonwealth," i.e., a community animated by concern for the common good and civic virtue, proposed by many of the founders of this nation. One commentator describes the tension as follows:

> The book's central theme is the erosion of the religious and republican communal ideals and the steady growth of the twin forms of individualism, often divided in one person between work (utilitarian individualism) and home, family and private life (expressive individualism). Without a vision and concern for the common good, the authors seem to say, the long-term survival of our society is in question.[48]

Jesus' reply to his enemies in today's Gospel implies that we owe Caesar more than taxes: The world, the human community has other rightful demands for our involvement and support. We cannot withdraw from our common life and social responsibilities into a narrow preoccupation with self-interest, or self-expression, or more intense and diverse experiences, or the safe isolation of small enclaves of people just like ourselves. The reign of God also calls for our involvement and our support.

The celebration of World Mission Sunday is a very appropriate reminder of what we owe to God. Like Cyrus, in the first reading, we are the Lord's anointed, called to be his servants and the instruments of his salvation. Called and anointed at baptism, confirmed by the Holy Spirit, nourished by the Eucharist, we are to be the people of that "complete conviction" which is faith, to proclaim God's glory among all the nations, among all peoples. We are to live by and for God, and to serve him, for he is the Lord, and there is no other. We do this by sharing our faith, personally, where we are, and everywhere through our care and concern and support for the missionary activities of the Church, keeping in mind that we receive from our brothers and sisters in other parts of the world even as we give. Every local church is both mission-sending and mission-receiving.

We live for God and we serve him by building his kingdom on earth, by promoting respect for the dignity of every human person, and by working for the well-being of every human community and for a lasting peace based on justice. The kingdom of God preached by Jesus defied every human privilege gained at the price of enslaving others or holding them in poverty, even when these privileges are ours not because of deliberate injustice on our part but only because of our continuing indifference or neglect or acceptance of the status quo. In this way what we owe to Caesar and what we owe to God come together if we, the Church, function adequately as a mediating institution that links individuals together with God's power and with the common good, with the needs of our society and of our world.

We can be this mediating institution, as a Christian community, if we are a place where persons feel loved, accepted, and free to be their unique selves while also challenging them to be part of a community of care. We can be this mediating institution if the church is a community in mission, engaged with the principalities and powers that deny the common good and promote isolated self-interest and isolating individualism, a community that empowers individuals to grow in active involvement and to be engaged in the promotion of the common good.

In the Eucharist we celebrate the death and resurrection of Jesus which gives us life and heals us of our brokenness and wounds, so that we might become healers and ministers of God's grace in a divided and broken world, so that it might become more completely one in Christ.

## Neighbors behind Walls

Time: October 28, 1984
Season: Thirtieth Sunday in Ordinary Time
Scripture Readings: Exodus 22:20–26;
  1 Thessalonians 1:5c–10; Matthew 22:34–40

Do you know the poem "Mending Wall" by Robert Frost? It begins like this:

> Something there is that doesn't love a wall,
> That sends the frozen-ground-swell under it
> And spills the upper boulders in the sun,
> And makes gaps even two can pass abreast.

Every year the winter freezes and hunters make big gaps in the wall that divides the poet's property from his neighbor's. Every spring the two get together to rebuild the wall, one on each side, a sort of outdoor game. "It comes to little more:" the poet continues:

> There where it is we do not need the wall:
> He is all pine and I am apple orchard.
> My apple trees will never get across
> And eat the cones under his pines, I tell him.
> He only says, "Good fences make good neighbors."
> Spring is the mischief in me, and I wonder
> If I could put a notion in his head:
> "*Why* do they make good neighbors? Isn't it
> Where there are cows? But here there are no cows.
> Before I built a wall I'd ask to know
> What I was walling in or walling out,
> And to whom I was like to give offense.
> Something there is that doesn't love a wall,
> That wants it down."

But the neighbor does not understand:

> He moves in darkness as it seems to me,
> Not of woods only and the shade of trees.
> He will not go behind his father's saying,
> And he likes having thought of it so well
> He says it again, "Good fences make good neighbors."

Do you believe that good fences make good neighbors? Here in the West we simply take it for granted that our property will be fenced in, perhaps because of the need to separate pasture from cultivated land, or the memory of conflicts between cattle ranchers and farmers, between cattlemen and sheepherders. Every time I travel in the East I notice the absence of fences.

I am inclined to agree with Robert Frost: Before building a wall to divide and separate we ought to know what we are walling out or walling in, what enmities we are creating, what divisions we are making permanent. I agree with the poet: "Something there is that doesn't love a wall, that wants it down." In a magnificent verse in the Letter to the Ephesians, speaking of the troublesome divisions and conflicts between Jews and Gentiles within the Christian community, Paul wrote: "For he [Christ] is our peace, who has made us both one, and has broken down the dividing wall of hostility..." (Eph. 2:14).

Today is Reformation Sunday. Our brothers and sisters in most Protestant churches are remembering and celebrating the beginning of the Reformation. Luther was said to have nailed his ninety-five theses against the misuse of indulgences to the door of the court church at Wittenberg on October 31, 1517. In many ways, nearly 500 years later we are still divided by a wall of hostility.

In the case of the Protestant denominations that have their roots in the reform movement that began with Luther or with the Anglican establishment—such as Lutherans, Episcopalians, Methodists, Presbyterians, and descendants of the radical Reformation, such as the Mennonites—there is no doubt in my mind that, to paraphrase Paul's words to the Ephesians, we share the same hope and faith and baptism, that there is only one Lord, one God and Father of us all, who is above all and through all and in all, that we are one body because it is the same Spirit that brings us all to life in Jesus Christ.

But we are not able to experience and celebrate that unity because we still mistrust each other's ministries and authority, and the ancient wounds have not been healed; the ancient enmities have not been reconciled. At the theological level, there is deep mutual respect and remarkable agreement on many of the doctrinal questions that divide us, but at the practical, emotional, personal, institutional level, we are still afraid of our differences, differences that should challenge and enrich us, not separate us. Our division is felt most painfully in the official prohibition to share the Eucharist, the celebration that is the sign and bond of Christian unity, the presence of the Lord himself who is our peace.

With some of the non-denominational forms of Protestantism, the more local and independent Christian churches, there are wider and, at least at this point, less-reconcilable differences. Many of these churches do not regard us Catholics as being Christian, because we have not been saved or "born again" according to their understanding of salvation. And at times I have difficulty recognizing the Jesus whom I confess as Lord and Savior in the Christ whom they preach. To my knowledge, there has been no serious dialogue between Roman Catholics and the more fundamentalist Christian groups, and here the division is deeper and the wounds more painful.

But this is precisely the revolutionary aspect of Jesus' great commandment of love, that the neighbor is not just the person who believes as I do, who belongs to the same ethnic group, who goes to the same church or even worships the same God. Jesus first unites love of God and love of neighbor, so that they are inseparable: You cannot have one without the other, and one is revealed and expressed in the other. Then he extends the concept of neighbor to include everyone, without exception. In the Gospel of Luke the scribes ask another question: Who is my neighbor? Jesus answers with the parable of the Good Samaritan who stops to care for his enemy.

Yes, we are to love even our enemies, those who hurt us or reject us, those who threaten us or oppress us. The first reading from Exodus suggests that even before Christ, God was already asking the Israelites to respect and care not only for their own people but also for the stranger, the alien in their midst. God's request, or command, is based on Israel's historical memories: They were aliens in the land of Egypt, where they were oppressed as slaves. Yahweh, in his great love for them, delivered them and set them free. Now they were to act the same way.

I would like to suggest that we, too, need to remember God's gracious love toward us, all that God has done for us, all the many ways in which God has revealed his kindness and care for us. We need to know, to believe, to feel, deep in the very heart of our being, how much God loves each of us, with all our differences and diversities, our contrasts, with all the ways in which all of us are at the same time like one another and unique.

It is only in being loved that our own power to love is released. In prayer, in God's holy word, in our coming together as God's people, in our personal story, we need to discover God's immense, unconditional love for us. Then we need to understand fully how God's love and fatherly care extend to everyone, without exception—to Protestants and Catholics, to Americans and Vietnamese and Hmong, even to Chinese communists. I believe it is a blasphemy against God's covenant love as revealed in Jesus Christ to exclude large portions of humanity from the possibility of salvation, of fullness of life in the glory of God. The possibility of that new life is rooted in the life, death, and resurrection of Jesus, but how that gift of new life is offered and accepted we must leave to the mystery of God's love for all his children.

If we really believe this—how much God loves each of us, without regard for what we are or what we do; how much God loves every human being and all his creatures without partiality—we will have taken the first and most important step toward loving our neighbor as ourselves.

## The Christian Hall of Fame

TIME: NOVEMBER 1, 1987
SEASON: THIRTY-FIRST SUNDAY IN ORDINARY TIME
  FEAST OF ALL SAINTS
SCRIPTURE READINGS: MALACHI 1:14B–2:2B, 8–10;
  1 THESSALONIANS 2:7B–9, 13; MATTHEW 23:1–12

Who are the heroes, the heroines, in your life today? Who are the models of behavior and life whom you try to imitate, whom you hold up for the admiration and imitation of the young people in your life? Be honest with yourself, and fill in the blank: "More than any other person I would want to be like_____."

Who are the heroes and heroines of our culture? All kinds of names ran through my mind when I asked myself this question. I wonder whom you are thinking of. Who are the people who have received media attention in recent years? Some people claim that the new heroes are the corporate executives. Others would say they are celebrities from the entertainment world, from the world of music, sports, movies, television. Others would point to politicians or televangelists. Our world seems to worship celebrity, not sanctity; personal success, not worthy accomplishments. In *Automatic Vaudeville*, John Lahr writes:

> Desperate efforts have been made to 'enshrine' individual accomplishments in Halls of Fame. Pantheons for strippers, baseball players, statesmen, cowboys, dog mushers, animal actors—nearly 750 Halls of Fame have been established (only three outside America) in a crude attempt to fix points of reference and cultural values.[49]

Maybe we need one more Hall of Fame, a Hall of Fame for Christians. Or maybe we have it already. Maybe that is what the Feast of All Saints is, in a strange way, because the saints we honor today do not have names. We do have many saints whom we honor by name, but today we rejoice with all those whose names are not remembered, but who also gave glory to God and brought goodness to our world. I am almost afraid to mention a Christian Hall of Fame for fear someone might think it is a good idea and start one, but do you have anyone you would like to nominate? Anyone you have known, living or dead, who is or was a faithful disciple of Jesus—especially when it was difficult and costly, a person who was committed and dedicated to God and his kingdom as Jesus was, joyful in the service of the Lord and of human beings, exuberant in the love of God, of life, of goodness.

What would be the requirements, the conditions, to be fulfilled for a place in this Christian Hall of Fame? I don't think we could do any better in setting down these requirements than the word of God in today's Gospel reading. The poor in spirit; the meek and the merciful; those who hunger and thirst for justice and are willing to suffer and be persecuted for the sake of what is holy and good, just, and right; the pure in heart who know how to put God first in their lives; the peacemakers: These are the ones whom God blesses, who share in the abundance of his life and happiness. These are the ones who belong in that Hall of Fame we call Heaven. I know, this looks like an impossible ideal, one that very few can attain. But Christian discipleship makes radical demands:

> The beatitudes are the outrageous expectations of an extravagant God. It is appropriate that God should set an impossible ideal for discipleship. Saints mirror God's immoderation. The Christian life is always moving toward an impossible dream in the confidence that God will not condemn us for missing the mark. That is what it means to take God at God's word.[50]

Do you want to try to make it into the Christian Hall of Fame? I really don't think we have a choice: We are all called to be saints, to be holy, because God is holy. And the Feast of All Saints need not depress us because it reminds us of how difficult the ideal is and how much we have failed. It should encourage us, because the saints whom we honor were all average human beings, with their fair share (at times even more than their fair share) of human frailties and failures, who, trusting in the love of God, did not give up. Today's feast should inspire us to want to be like them, to be holy.

In one of his sermons, Saint Bernard captured the meaning of the feast. He said:

> The saints have no need of honor from us; neither does our devotion add the slightest thing to what is theirs. Clearly, if we venerate their memory, it serves us, not them. I feel myself inflamed by a tremendous yearning.[51]

Do you feel a tremendous yearning to have a part in the happiness, the peace, the fulfillment promised by the Gospel? We can, we will. We are already the children of God, and if we try to live as his children, we will be part of that huge crowd beyond numbering from every nation, race, people, and tongue, gathered before the throne of God in the great heavenly liturgy.

May our liturgy here this morning be for us a beginning and a foreshadowing of that heavenly liturgy, and may the praise, honor, glory, and thanksgiving which we offer today be joined with that of the saints in heaven, as we ourselves hope to be joined with them one day in the fullness of life with God.

## Come to the Party!

TIME: NOVEMBER 11, 1990
SEASON: THIRTY-SECOND SUNDAY IN ORDINARY TIME
SCRIPTURE READINGS: WISDOM 6:12–16;
1 THESSALONIANS 4:13–18; MATTHEW 25:1–13

I would like to focus your attention on the second reading and on the Gospel. Because of the way many of us have been trained to hear these texts, our first reaction would be to think they are both talking about the same thing: death, how we should feel about those who have died and being ready for our own death. But that is not completely correct.

Paul's first letter to the Thessalonians is the first written document of the Christian faith. There were probably other texts written before this, but this letter is the first Christian writing that has come down to us as part of the official, canonical, normative Christian Scriptures, what we call the New Testament. This writing preceded the first written Gospel by perhaps twenty years, and it was written less than twenty years after the death of Jesus.

I think it is extremely important for us to know this, because it tells us that from the very beginning of the Christian religious experience, the faith of the original disciples of Jesus reflected a belief in the resurrection—not only for Christ, but for ourselves as well. Those who believe in Christ will be raised up from the dead as Jesus was, to share his risen life. This belief, therefore, is not the conclusion of a long process of faith development and theological discussion as is, for example, the doctrine of the Trinity. The belief that we share in the resurrection of Jesus is primordial, immediate, foundational, embedded into the most primitive, original experience of faith. Death has no final power over us, because we are destined to share fullness of life in the Risen Christ. That is why we cannot "yield to grief as if we had no hope." Those who have "fallen asleep" ahead of us, those who have preceded us in death, will be brought forth to life by God, as will we, and we will all be together for eternity. We are to console one another with this message.

The message is expressed in the framework of the images and expectations prevalent in Paul's time. This is a primitive stage of faith. Paul, and the Thessalonians, were convinced that the Parousia, the return of Jesus in glory to establish the fullness of God's kingdom, would happen very soon, in their own lifetime. That is why the Thessalonians were concerned and had asked Paul about the fate of those who had died before the Parousia: Would they share in the glory of the Lord? And Paul reassures them that indeed they would. (By the end of his life, Paul had begun to realize that the Parousia would not be coming soon, and to think of his death as a separate event that would happen first.)

Paul also uses traditional images to try to describe what this being "raised up" would mean: coming down and going up, sounds of trumpets and angelic voices, ascent into clouds. These images don't work for a lot of people today, although they do for some, for those who read the Scriptures literally. This is the passage people use when they talk about the "rapture": The rapture is being caught up into the clouds of heaven to be with Jesus. I remember seeing a bumper sticker: "In case of the rapture, this car will be unmanned." Thanks a lot, I thought. You are snatched up to meet the Lord in the clouds, and your car crashes into me!

Martin Marty, a Lutheran historian and theologian, uses a contemporary image. He describes being struck by this phrase in *Scientific American:* "Does a black hole lie at the center of our galaxy?" The image of the black hole, "a collapsed mass so dense that nothing can escape its gravitational field, even light," becomes for him a metaphor of the human condition. None of us can ever escape the gravitational pull of the field, the black hole, that we know as death. In the black hole, even light gets pulled in and overcome. Does the meaning of life become void, the light extinguished, in the dark density of death?

Marty responds to that question with the answer of faith: The word of God, the Word made flesh in Jesus, his life, death, and resurrection, give meaning to our life and link us to the ultimate meaning, God, who cannot be pulled in by the black hole of death. Our darkness has been overcome in Jesus: "In him was life, and this life was the light of all. The light shines in darkness, and the darkness has not overcome it" (John 1:4-5)—not even the black hole of death.

Ultimately, however, we have no adequate images of resurrection and life after death. I agree with the theologians who argue—and it is pure speculation—that the unity of spirit and matter in our human reality is so essential to what we are that whatever transformation of this spirit and matter is to take place, it must happen with death, so that resurrection is not an event at the end of history and the present world, but just on the other side of life as we know it. But the crucial element is that original conviction that in some way all of us are called to share in the resurrection and new life in Christ, and that those who have gone before us will be part of our future life. This is the consolation that Christian faith offers us, from the very beginning even until now.

In the time remaining, I want to make one important point about today's Gospel reading: We cannot limit the idea of being ready to welcome the Lord to the moment of our death. That is not what the Gospel is saying. It is the kingdom of God that is like the parable of the ten maidens who are waiting for the coming of the bridegroom. And the kingdom of God begins here and now. The Lord comes into our life every day, in a variety of ways, if only we are willing to look and listen, to be awake and alert, ready to welcome him and to follow him. The kingdom of God comes to be when the hungry are fed, and the thirsty given water, and the sick comforted, and the homeless given shelter, and the oppressed set free.

The bridegroom comes to us in our sisters and brothers in need. The kingdom of God is being built up whenever and wherever our human capacities and those of our brothers and sisters are encouraged and empowered and brought closer to fulfillment, all our physical, psychological, spiritual capacities, all our creative, feeling, knowing, loving, giving powers. We do not have to wait for death: The Lord Jesus, the bridegroom, comes to us now, and his creative transformation is at work in us to shape us into full human beings now, to lead us to the fullness of human life, the life that he lived, the life that he made possible for us by his death and resurrection. This is the best way to prepare for death; this is the best way to get ready for his final coming in glory. Both then and now, Matthew says, when the party starts you want to be on the right side of the door!

## Multiplying Our Talents

TIME: NOVEMBER 18, 1984
SEASON: THIRTY-THIRD SUNDAY IN ORDINARY TIME
SCRIPTURE READINGS: PROVERBS 31:10–13, 19–20, 30–31;
1 THESSALONIANS 5:1–6; MATTHEW 25:14–30

Most of us are neither brilliantly learned and wise nor wealthy and powerful, but we are the only ones the Lord has to take care of things until he returns. He left both his creation and his kingdom in our care. All that is, all that has life belongs to him, but we are responsible for the portion that he has entrusted to us.

In understanding the Bible, especially the Gospels, I find it very helpful to look at the way the stories developed, how the preaching and the telling of the stories modified and adapted them, until they became available to the Gospel authors, who used them for their individual purposes, adapted them to their own faith vision and theological understanding. I would like to look at today's Gospel in that way.

At the Jesus level, when Jesus told the story, it was taken from real life; it reflected something that happened at the time of Jesus. A rich man is going on a long journey and he entrusts his money to three servants, according to their ability, so that it would not remain idle during his absence. We are talking about a lot of money: The talent was a measure of weight that became the highest denomination of coin. We have to think in terms of millions of dollars to get the picture. Historically, the bankers in Jerusalem paid excellent rates of interest on money entrusted to them by merchants. A rudimentary form of insurance was even available! Profits came from foreign trade, and they were high because the Romans kept trade routes safe from pirates and hijackers.

Two of the servants in today's story did very well with their master's money: 100 percent gain! The third one, cautious and afraid, simply protected what he had received and gave it back to the owner. The master is very harsh on this third servant. He rebukes him and takes away his trust. How did Jesus apply this true-life story? He probably used it to condemn the Jewish religious authorities who were like the third servant: They were so careful to preserve the purity of the tradition that had been entrusted to them that they were not open to new situations and circumstances; they were unable to hear the message of Jesus and refused to accept it.

In the remembering and interpretation of the early Christian community, the parable was moralized by the addition of the proverb: "To everyone who has, God will give; but from him who has not, he will take away what he has." And the parable is applied to the new situation of the Christian believer: The master is understood as Christ, the departure is the Ascension of Jesus, and the delayed return is the Parousia, reflecting the expectation of the imminent return of Jesus in glory. The words "enter into the joy of the Lord" make the reward sound like the participation in the messianic banquet at the end of time. The story assumes an apocalyptic flavor. The moral is that we must work and do the best we can while we wait for the return of Christ in glory.

The setting of the parable in Matthew's Gospel points more directly to Christians and to the leaders of Christian communities. The Parousia seems even more remote, and structures of church leadership are developing. Matthew has a special concern that the emerging leaders in the church not look for honor and privilege, but be humble servants. The reliable servant for Matthew is the Christian, and especially the Christian leader who hears the teaching of Christ and does it. Next Sunday's Gospel will give us the verses immediately following today's reading, the scene of the great judgment based on how well we have responded to the needs of our brothers and sisters.

What does the story say to us today? How do you interpret it? What did it say to you? What were your thoughts during the reading and when it was finished? If we take the original meaning of the story, if we are able to hear what Jesus was first trying to say, perhaps we will discover an analogy between the servant who is afraid and hides the money in the ground and people in the church, in society, who are afraid of change and oppose anything new, who insist on traditional values as a way of ignoring new ideas and realities, who cling to the past in order to avoid the challenges of the present. Of course, genuine values of the past must be preserved, but clinging to the past may indicate a desire for false security and a lack of adventurous obedience to the will of God here and now. Does that apply to us?

Paul, in the second reading, also warns us about a false sense of security that will come crashing down when we least expect it, and he exhorts us not to be asleep. Are we awake to the coming of the Lord in our life here and now? Are we aware of the movement of the Spirit in our time? Are we willing to hear the message of Jesus for us and to follow him wherever he may lead us?

The interpretation of the early Christian community in reference to the return of the Lord in glory fits the liturgical use of the text. During this month of November the Church wants us to focus on the mystery of death and the consummation of history in the final establishment of the fullness of God's kingdom. These are apocalyptic themes; they raise the question of the end of time. The early Christians expected the Lord to return very soon, in their own lifetime, but he was not coming; he was delaying his return. There was only one thing to do: continue to work faithfully at one's tasks, use one's gifts and abilities for the sake of the Lord, adding to what belongs to him, to his kingdom.

There are people today who expect the end of time, the rapture, to come very soon. But the reality is that we have no way of knowing "specific times and moments." We continue to live our life, the times and moments that God has given us; we continue to do our work, to take care of our responsibilities faithfully and well, like the valiant woman, the worthy wife of the first reading, reaching out to the poor, extending our arms to the needy. The Lord has entrusted his world and his kingdom to us—even his heart, his love for the world and for his people. We must make it grow, and bloom, and bear fruit.

The way Matthew uses the parable forces me to stop and look at myself and my ministry. As a pastor of a Christian community, I am one of the leaders who were of concern to Matthew. Am I looking for privileges, for titles and honors for myself, for my own glory? Or am I truly a servant of God's people, not just in words but in deeds? Am I serving my own gain or the glory of God and his kingdom? More and more of you are going to be called to positions of leadership and ministry in Christian communities. These questions are crucial.

And I hear the parable in yet another way. I see the servant who buries his treasure as a metaphor of the tendency in our society to hoard our gifts, to hang on to what we have, to refuse to share it and put it to good use for the benefit of others, for the common good. I see the wicked servant as an image of the tendency to worry only about ourselves, to take care of our own needs, to be safe and secure in our own little world, and to ignore the needs of our communities and of our brothers and sisters.

I believe God expects us to speculate, as did the two successful servants, to gamble, to take risks, to use and test our gifts, our abilities, our time and energy, our material resources, to the very limit, not for ourselves but for him and for his kingdom. And then we can wait for his return not in fear, but with hope and with joy.

## Will You Be Part of the Kingdom?

Time: November 22, 1987
Season: Christ the King
Scripture Readings: Ezekiel 34: 11–12, 15–17;
1 Corinthians 15:20–26, 28; Matthew 25:31–46

It has been said that the most efficient form of government is a benevolent dictatorship—a government headed by one person with the authority to make final decisions, who has the best interests of all the people at heart. But such a ruler would consult with and seek advice from the wisest minds and kindest hearts, would weigh all the elements of a decision with the greatest care, would make the choice that is right and just and good for all the people, and would have the power to implement his decisions without waste of time or resources.

When I describe it like that, it almost sounds tempting, doesn't it? Especially when we see the dark side of democratic governments—the inefficiency, the waste, the inability to make critical and urgent decisions, either because of a lack of leadership or because of insoluble conflicts between strong-willed, stubborn leaders, the risk of a country becoming like a ship tossed by the storms with no one at the helm. There is only one little problem: Benevolent dictatorships are practically impossible to find. Once in control, a dictator has only one thing in mind: self-survival in power at all costs. I know of only one benevolent king, one absolute ruler who fits the description I gave above: Jesus Christ.

The Scripture readings present a magnificent sweep of time and space as they give a number of rich images to describe both the absolute power of God over all creation, and the way he exercises that power. In the first reading, the Israelites are exiles in Babylon. In their pride and complacency they never thought that God would allow this terrible disaster to come upon them. But now the city and the temple have been destroyed and there are no leaders left—no king, no priests. God, speaking through Ezekiel, condemns the "shepherds" of Israel, the kings who had refused to accept God's word and brought disaster to their people. He then promises that his people will return to their land: God will become their shepherd again, rescuing, gathering, healing, caring for them tenderly in a new covenant of peace.

This image is continued in Psalm 23, and it recurs in the Gospel. Here we have moved from historical circumstances to the end of history. In this final parable in Matthew's Gospel, the shepherd king, now identified as Jesus, sits on the throne of judgment, surrounded by his court, ready to share the glory of his kingdom with those who are worthy of it. And who are those lucky people? Not those who served the king with heroic deeds, or those who sacrificed their lives in the great battles for his kingdom; not even those who held positions of great responsibility in his kingdom on earth. No, they are those whose deeds of mercy match the very mercy of the king, those who have acted with kindness and concern toward the poor, the sick, the homeless, the prisoners, the strangers, all the "least ones," for the king, the Christ, has chosen to identify himself with the least of his brothers and sisters.

I would like to underline the all-inclusive universality of this great scene of judgment. The parable speaks of "the nations" being gathered before Christ's royal throne. In the Scriptures, this phrase refers to the whole world, especially the pagan world, not just the chosen people, the believers. In the past we have been too prone to identify the kingdom of God with the Church, to say that if you do not belong to the Church, if you do not believe as we do, you do not belong to the kingdom, and therefore you are not saved. That is clearly wrong. The kingdom of God and the Church are two different realities. Everyone is called to the kingdom of God, and the kingdom of God is present wherever and whenever people act kindly and mercifully and lovingly toward one another.

Some, always a minority, are called by God to be his people, to be the instruments, the signs, the concrete expression of the kingdom in history. This is the Church, the community of those who know and believe in Jesus. But if we fail to live the reality of the kingdom in our life, to do mercy and to act kindly and to walk humbly, we will have no special claim to the inheritance of the kingdom. There will be many who have never even heard of Christ who will discover that in fact they are part of his kingdom. And there will be those who will say: "We heard your word, we sat at your table!" to whom the Lord will answer: "I do not know you!"

In the second reading, Paul goes the final step beyond the judgment of human history described in the Gospel. Now it is the whole of creation that is brought into unity under the dominion of Christ. All antagonistic powers have been subdued; all enemies have been conquered—even the last enemy, death; all differences and contrasts are held together in a harmony of richness and variety. All is now moving in one direction under the leadership of Christ; everything is now responding fully and joyfully to the invitation and the empowering of God's love; all is centered and made one in Christ, and Christ turns everything over to the Father, so that God may be all in all.

This is the kingdom to which we are invited to belong; this is the king to whom we are asked to give our obedience, our loyalty, our service, our devotion, our love: Christ, who is in our midst as one who serves, as shepherd and guide, as word of invitation, as bread of life, who wants to lead us to the ultimate fullness of God's kingdom.

I invite you to pray with me the prayer of St. Ignatius:

Take, Lord, receive all my liberty,
my memory, my understanding, my entire will—
all that I have and call my own.
You have given it all to me.
To you, Lord, I return it.
Everything is yours.
Do with it what you will.
Give me only your love and your grace.
That is enough for me.

# Notes

# Notes

1. Gerald S. Sloyan, "Serving the Word," *Homily Service: An Ecumenical Resource for Sharing the Word*, Washington, D.C., The Liturgical Conference, 31:9 (Dec. 1998), p. 40.
2. See Barbara Brown Taylor, "Believing the Impossible," in *Gospel Medicine*, Boston, Mass.: Cowley Publications, 1995, pp. 155, 157.
3. Story from Jose Antonio Rubio, "Serving the Word," *Homily Service: An Ecumenical Resource for Sharing the Word*, Washington, D.C.: The Liturgical Conference, 31:9 (Dec. 1998), pp. 59–60.
4. "Homily Model," *Good News*, New Berlin, Wis.: Liturgical Publications, 16:12 (Dec. 1989), p. 480.
5. *Ibid.*
6. Joseph T. Nolan, "Letter from the Editor," *Good News*, New Berlin, Wis.: Liturgical Publications, 17:1 (Jan. 1990), p. 2.
7. This homily is appropriate for the Sunday before Ash Wednesday, regardless of when it falls. The homily is not based on the appointed readings for the day, but is an invitation to celebrate the goodness of life—and even be a bit foolish.
8. Patricia Aberdene and John Naisbitt, *The Fresno Bee*, 8 March 1993.
9. *Homily Service: An Ecumenical Resource for Sharing the Word*, Washington, D.C., The Liturgical Conference, 20:1, (Apr. 1987), p. 20.
10. *Ibid.*
11. *Ibid.*
12. At the beginning of this homily, Fr. Negro cites John J. O'Donnell, "The Cross in a Secular World," *Commonweal*, CII:8 (Apr. 9, 1974), pp. 234–236.
13. H. Richard Niebuhr, *The Kingdom of God in America*. New York: Harper and Row, 1959, p. 193.

14. *Newsweek,* Apr. 8, 1996, pp. 60-70.
15. *Ibid.,* p. 62.
16. *Ibid.,* p. 65.
17. Marcus Borg, *Jesus: A New Vision,* quoted in Luke Timothy Johnson, *The Real Jesus: The Misguided Quest for the Historical Jesus and the Truth of the Traditional Gospels.* San Francisco: Harper San Francisco, 1996, p. 40. According to Geza Vermes, *Jesus the Jew,* Jesus also was a charismatic figure, a chasid, whose disciples believed he was the Messiah, as has happened even in our own time. (Johnson, p. 36).
18. Reginald H. Fuller, *Preaching the New Lectionary: The Word of God for the Church Today.* Collegeville, Minn.: The Liturgical Press, 1974, p. 189.
19. *Homily Service: An Ecumenical Resource for Sharing the Word,* Washington, D.C., The Liturgical Conference, 20:2 (May 1987), p. 31.
20. *Panthiesme et Christianisme,* 1923, p. 12. Quoted in Christopher Mooney, *Teilhard de Chardin and the Mystery of Christ.* New York: Harper and Row, 1964, p. 82.
21. *Hymn of the Universe.* New York: Harper and Row, 1965, pp. 24–25, 34, 37.
22. *Good News,* New Berlin, Wis.: Liturgical Publications, 14:6 (June 1987), p. 222.
23. Irene Nowell, *Sing a New Song: The Psalms in the Sunday Lectionary.* Collegeville, Minn.: The Liturgical Press, 1993, pp. 293–294.
24. The Roman Creed says: "Credo in Spiritum Sanctum . . . qui ex Patre Filioque procedit (I believe in the Holy Spirit who proceeds from the Father and the Son). The Orthodox leave out Filioque (and the Son): the Holy Spirit proceeds only from the Father, not from the Son.
25. "Studying the Lectionary," *Homily Service: An Ecumenical Resource for Sharing the Word,* Washington, D.C.: The Liturgical Conference, 23:3 (June 1990), p. 27.

26. The word translated as "feed" [eat] in today's passage literally means "to gnaw." Arthur J. Dewey, "Scriptural Commentary for June," *Good News,* New Berlin, Wis.: Liturgical Publications, 17:6 (June 1990), p. 220.
27. Quoted by Walter J. Burghardt, S. J., *Sir, We Would Like to See Jesus: Homilies from a Hilltop.* New York: Paulist Press, 1982, p. 160.
28. Quoted in Thomas H. Stahel, "Man hu (a.k.a. Manna, a.k.a. Bread of Angels)," *America,* 162:22 (June 9, 1990), p. 591.
29. Henri J. M. Nouwen, *Reaching Out: The Three Movements of the Spiritual Life.* Garden City, NY: Doubleday and Company, 1975, p. 46.
30. *Ibid.,* p. 73.
31. "Studying the Lectionary," *Homily Service: An Ecumenical Resource for Sharing the Word,* Washington, D.C.: The Liturgical Conference, 19:4 (July 1996), p. 18.
32. Cardinal Joseph Bernardin, "Reflections on 'moral crisis' gripping medical profession," *American Medical News,* Feb. 5, 1996, p. 18.
33. *Journal of a Soul,* trans. Dorothy White, New York: McGraw-Hill, 1965, pp. 278-79.
34. *The Four Quartets,* quoted in Richard Foster, *Freedom of Simplicity.* San Francisco: Harper and Row, 1981, p. 94.
35. *Christian Perfection,* p. 204, quoted in Foster, *op. cit.,* p. 93.
36. "Studying the Lectionary," *Homily Service: An Ecumenical Resource for Sharing the Word,* Washington, D.C.: The Liturgical Conference, 23:5 (Aug. 1990), p. 4.
37. *Ibid.,* p. 9.
38. *Share the Word,* 8:4, July–Aug. 1987, pp. 75–79, passim.
39. "Studying the Lectionary," *Homily Service: An Ecumenical Resource for Sharing the Word,* Washington, D.C.: The Liturgical Conference, 20:5 (Aug. 1987), p. 14.

40. Sharon H. Ringe, "A Gentile Woman's Story," in *Feminist Interpretation of the Bible*, ed. Letty M. Russell, Philadelphia: Westminster Press, 1985, p. 7.

41. In *The Church: Readings in Theology*, compiled by The Canisianum, Innsbruck, New York, NY: P.J. Kennedy and Sons, 1963, pp. 3-15.

42. *Ibid.*, p. 4.

43. *Enarrationes* in Ps. 99, 11 (PL 37, 1278). Quoted in Rahner, *The Church: Readings in Theology, op. cit.*, p. 8.

44. Joseph T. Nolan, "Preaching Commentary," *Good News*, New Berlin, Wis.: Liturgical Publications, 14:9 (Sept. 1987), p. 328. For the story of Henry Poels, see Gerald P. Fogarty, "Dissent at Catholic University: The Case of Henry Poels," *America*, 156:9, pp. 180-184.

45. Jim Forest, "On the love of enemies," *Living Prayer*, 29:2 (Mar.–Apr. 1996), pp. 14-17.

46. In the Gospel of Matthew, "kingdom of heaven" is a euphemism for "the kingdom of God." Matthew, as a good Jew, is reluctant to use the name of God.

47. "Ideas and Illustrations," *Homily Service: An Ecumenical Resource for Sharing the Word*, Washington, D. C. : The Liturgical Conference, 27:7 (Oct. 1996), p. 25.

48. *Homily Service: An Ecumenical Resource for Sharing the Word*, Washington, D. C. : The Liturgical Conference, 20:7 (Oct. 1987), p. 19.

49. Quoted in Gary Siebert, "Saints Alive!," in *America*, "The Word," 157:11 (Oct. 24, 1987), p. 279.

50. *Homily Service: An Ecumenical Resource for Sharing the Word*, Washington, D. C. : The Liturgical Conference, 20:8 (Nov. 1987), p. 11.

51. Quoted in *Good News*, New Berlin, Wis.: Liturgical Publications, 14:11 (Nov. 1987), p. 386.

# Index

# Index

## A

Advent 1, 4-6, 9, 10, 12, 14, 20, 30, 44, 155
Apocalyptic 1, 217, 218
Ascension 113, 217
Authority 4, 10, 153, 168, 169, 177, 178, 180, 190, 205, 220

## B

Baptism 36-38, 40-43, 45, 60, 86, 87, 93, 95, 100, 101, 109, 118, 159, 202, 205
Bible 30, 98, 100, 117, 123, 144, 148, 186, 216
Biblical 36, 41, 66, 88, 90, 97, 139, 141, 142, 144, 145, 149, 167, 168, 170, 185, 188, 201
Blessed 24, 30, 52, 79, 101, 111, 121, 124, 135, 173
Blood 60, 78, 79, 86, 96, 125-127, 137, 198
Body 30, 40, 53, 65, 78, 79, 86, 91, 92, 96, 102, 108, 114, 119, 125-127, 163, 171, 182, 205
Bread 25, 55, 74, 78, 79, 95-98, 100, 101, 107, 125-127, 157-159, 161, 170, 222

## C

Calling 4, 45, 46, 91, 177, 190
Catholic(s) 10, 29, 30, 37, 54, 55, 87, 102, 108, 109, 120, 159, 168, 169, 171, 178, 180, 191, 197, 206, 207
Celebrate, celebration 17, 19, 20, 32, 43, 54-57, 60, 69, 76, 78, 79, 86-88, 95, 97, 98, 100, 106, 109, 112, 113, 117-119, 127-129, 148, 182, 198, 202, 203, 205, 206
Charismatic 90, 118
Choice 10, 29, 41, 42, 53, 58, 59, 61, 63, 65, 70, 82, 122, 143, 154-156, 174, 199, 209, 220
Christ 1, 6, 7, 10-12, 19-21, 30, 33-35, 40-43, 48, 52, 55, 57, 59, 63, 65, 73, 74, 77, 78, 80, 84, 87, 88, 90-93, 96, 100, 106, 108, 109, 111-114, 116, 118, 119, 125-127, 129, 132, 137, 144, 145, 149, 152, 158, 159, 163, 165, 166, 168, 170, 171, 182, 183, 185, 191, 192, 194, 195, 197-199, 203, 205-207, 212, 214, 217, 220-222
Christian(s) 2, 4, 6, 10, 29, 32, 33, 36, 37, 41, 48, 50, 52, 54, 55-57, 61, 80, 82, 84, 86-88, 90, 91, 95, 97, 98, 102, 103, 105, 107-111, 118, 123, 126, 131-133, 136, 139, 144, 145, 155, 158, 159, 164, 169, 170, 173, 176, 182, 183, 185, 190-192, 194, 196, 197, 202, 205, 206, 208, 209, 212, 214, 217-219
Christmas 1, 14, 17, 20, 22, 23, 25, 27, 41, 44, 45, 117, 123
Church(es) 10-13, 28-30, 37, 38, 44, 48, 54-56, 66, 69, 73, 87, 88, 93, 95-97, 100, 102, 103, 106-109, 116-118, 129-131, 138, 144, 146, 153, 159, 168-171, 177, 178, 180-183, 185, 187, 191, 194, 196, 197, 199, 200, 202, 205, 206, 217, 218, 221
Comfort 4, 25, 62, 103, 118, 132, 162

Community  4, 6, 11, 12, 20, 28, 29, 33, 36, 42, 47, 50, 51, 55, 70, 75, 87, 91, 93, 95-98, 100, 103, 107-110, 116, 119, 123, 124, 127, 131, 132, 139, 144-146, 153, 162-164, 169, 178, 181, 183, 185, 187, 189-191, 196, 198, 201-203, 205, 217-219, 221

Compassion  20, 67, 73, 91, 96, 131, 132, 148, 166, 171, 185

Confess(ion)  7, 43, 73, 74, 84, 150, 161, 166, 168, 206

Covenant  2, 4, 30, 33, 34, 85, 86, 121, 125, 167, 171, 190, 191, 207, 221

Creation  1, 5, 6, 24, 26, 34, 40, 52, 58, 76, 85-87, 90, 106, 114, 116, 148, 158, 159, 216, 220, 222

Cross  24, 30, 60-63, 65, 66, 80, 82-86, 88, 98, 102, 123, 126, 140, 170, 173, 174, 176, 192

# D

Death  2, 10, 12, 13, 17, 21, 25, 27, 37, 57-63, 65, 73, 74, 76, 77, 79, 80, 82-88, 90, 92, 97, 100, 103, 110, 114, 123, 137, 143, 153, 158, 161, 169, 170, 174, 176, 182, 187, 188, 190, 192, 193, 195, 197, 198, 203, 207, 212-215, 218, 222

Desert  45, 59, 79, 85, 86, 116, 118, 125, 161, 173

Disciple(ship)  11, 41, 46, 52, 68, 69, 87, 91, 174, 176, 191, 209

# E

Eternal life  76, 123, 186, 197

Eternity  182, 213

Eucharist  30, 43, 55, 74, 78, 79, 95-98, 100, 112, 114, 116, 126-128, 130, 158-160, 198, 202, 203, 206

Evil  21, 23, 46, 58, 65, 79, 92, 104, 111, 150, 152, 155, 188

# F

Faith  2, 4, 10, 11, 16, 17, 21, 24, 28-30, 33, 34, 36, 56, 58, 63, 73, 77, 83, 85-88, 90-93, 95-97, 100, 105, 110-112, 114, 116, 123, 126, 127, 133, 136, 144-146, 158, 159, 162-166, 168-171, 190, 192, 194, 198, 199, 202, 205, 212-214, 216

Family  1, 6, 7, 14, 16, 17, 25, 28-30, 35, 37, 38, 47, 56, 66, 86, 87, 92, 112, 117, 127, 139, 146, 183, 185, 187, 200, 201

Feed, food  6, 52, 56, 107, 108, 125-127, 129, 139, 159, 163, 168, 199

Forgive(ness)  12, 24, 96, 118, 130, 152, 181-183, 185

Freedom  5, 6, 13, 14, 47, 70, 86, 112, 138, 140, 141, 155, 178, 180, 188, 192

#

Gift  12, 24, 25, 27, 67, 72, 78, 79, 93, 95, 104, 106, 117, 118, 123, 125-127, 132, 157, 167, 172, 188, 198, 199, 207

God  2, 4, 7, 11, 12, 14, 16, 17, 19-21, 23, 24, 26, 27, 30, 32-34, 36-38, 40, 42-48, 50-53, 56-63, 65, 67, 68, 70, 72-74, 76-78, 80, 82-88, 90-93, 95-98, 100-102, 104,

# Index

105, 107-109, 112-114, 117-126, 129-133, 136, 137, 139, 140, 144-146, 148-150, 152-158, 161-167, 169-171, 173, 177, 178, 181-183, 186-189, 191-195, 197-200, 202, 205-210, 212-214, 217-222
Good News    12, 13, 27, 34, 45, 67, 88, 95, 96, 107, 108, 118, 144, 167, 197
Grace    11, 25, 27, 40, 41, 59, 65, 69, 87, 96, 111, 113, 137, 153, 188, 189, 198, 203, 222

## H

Healing    13, 25, 46, 165, 166, 183, 192, 221
Hebrew(s)    42, 58, 72, 80, 107, 117, 125, 127, 139, 164, 178, 183
History    1, 10, 34, 36, 51, 52, 58, 72, 73, 80, 83-86, 90, 91, 100, 106, 108, 116, 122, 136, 138-140, 153, 155, 158, 159, 163, 169, 170, 196, 214, 218, 221, 222
Holy Spirit    16, 77, 106, 118, 119, 123, 124, 183, 202
Homeless    25, 140, 159, 214, 221
Hope    11-13, 20, 22, 25, 26, 28, 30, 32, 34, 35, 50, 56, 76, 77, 87, 90, 93, 101, 111-113, 116, 118, 119, 136, 137, 140, 142, 144, 146, 148, 150, 155, 157, 159, 167, 189, 192, 205, 210, 212, 219
Hospitality    139-141
Humility    50, 53, 142, 143, 180

## I

Incarnation    116
Inspiration    22
Inspire    92, 209

## J

Jesus    1, 2, 4-6, 10-14, 16, 19, 20, 22, 29, 33-38, 40-43, 45-48, 51, 52, 55, 57, 59-63, 65-69, 72- 78, 82-85, 88, 90-93, 95-98, 100-114, 118, 121, 123, 124, 126, 127, 129, 130, 132, 137, 143-145, 148-150, 152, 154, 155, 158, 159, 161-168, 170, 173, 174, 176, 181-183, 185-187, 190-200, 202, 203, 205-207, 209, 212-218, 220, 221
Jews, Jewish    2, 10, 29, 30, 32-34, 45, 66, 75, 78, 85, 107, 110, 111, 118, 126, 165-167, 190, 191, 194, 195, 200, 205, 217
Justice    6, 30, 46, 50, 65, 82, 102, 112, 122, 138, 139, 148, 177, 194, 199, 202, 209

## K

Kingdom (of God)    7, 10-12, 38, 45, 46, 48, 55, 69, 79, 80, 86, 90, 106, 142, 145, 146, 148, 149, 153, 155, 167, 173, 186-189, 191-194, 202, 209, 213, 214, 216, 218-222

## L

Law    2, 12, 14, 42, 66, 72, 86, 118-120, 171, 186, 191, 197

Lent   30, 44, 50, 53, 58, 61, 62, 66, 70, 75-77, 155
Life   1, 2, 10, 12, 13, 16, 17, 22-26, 28, 30, 34, 36, 40-44, 46-48, 52-58, 60-63, 65, 66, 68, 75-80, 82, 86-88, 90-93, 95-98, 100, 101, 103-107, 109-113, 117-120, 122-124, 126, 127, 129-132, 135-140, 143, 144, 146, 148, 150, 152-159, 161-163, 170, 171, 173, 174, 176, 182, 183, 185-187, 189-192, 194, 195, 197, 199, 201, 203, 205, 207-210, 212-218, 221, 222
Liturgy, liturgical   1, 30, 41-45, 70, 78, 87, 93, 97, 106, 117, 123, 131-133, 140, 142, 148, 157, 163, 191, 210, 218
Love   7, 11-13, 17, 19-21, 24-26, 29, 32-34, 38, 43, 46, 56, 57, 61, 63, 65, 68-70, 73, 77, 79, 87, 91, 92, 96, 105, 108, 110-112, 114, 117, 121, 123, 124, 127-132, 148, 149, 154, 157-160, 163, 166, 167, 170, 171, 176, 178, 180, 182, 185, 188, 195, 197-199, 204-207, 209, 218, 222

# M

Marriage   17, 44, 76, 78, 86, 112
Mass   43, 102, 116, 127, 129, 132, 138, 191, 213
Mercy   11, 43, 73, 129-132, 166, 167, 183, 185, 188, 221
Messiah   67, 77, 102, 142, 145, 166
Ministry   2, 38, 42, 45, 59, 65, 69, 79, 82, 95, 106, 110, 150, 152, 161, 187, 219
Miracle(s)   73, 75, 163

Mission   12, 13, 36, 37, 42, 59, 67, 82, 107, 109, 118, 123, 136, 165, 166, 169, 202
Money   61, 157, 186-188, 195, 200, 201, 216, 217

# N

Nation   6, 11, 35, 109, 140, 143, 157, 167, 185, 201, 210
Nature   70, 145

# P

Pain   16, 17, 26, 53, 58-60, 63, 65, 73, 80, 82, 167, 173, 177
Parable   144, 145, 149, 181, 183, 186-188, 191, 194, 196, 197, 199, 206, 214, 217, 219, 221
Parousia   62, 213, 217
Peace   6, 7, 9, 20, 24-26, 46-48, 56, 61, 73, 87, 96, 112, 118, 121, 124, 130, 131, 142, 148, 156, 182, 195, 202, 205, 206, 210, 221
People   1, 2, 4, 6, 7, 11-14, 16, 17, 20, 28, 32-38, 40, 42, 44-47, 50, 51, 53-56, 58-60, 67, 68, 70, 72, 75, 76, 78, 83, 85-87, 90, 95, 96, 100, 104, 107, 109-111, 113, 116-120, 125, 127, 130, 131, 133, 138, 139, 142, 143, 146, 149, 150, 154, 155, 157-161, 165, 167, 169, 171, 173, 176-178, 181-183, 185, 187, 190, 191, 193, 197, 201, 202, 206-208, 210, 213, 217-221
Poor   7, 13, 24, 35, 47, 50-53, 112, 119, 132, 139, 142, 167, 187, 192-194, 209, 218, 221

*Index* 235

Pope  10, 96, 156, 171, 177, 178, 180
Poverty  7, 17, 50, 51, 53, 77, 139, 140, 162, 202
Power  4, 5, 12, 20, 21, 23, 27, 36-38, 40, 51, 53, 54, 59-61, 63, 65, 67, 68, 82, 84-87, 92, 101-105, 107-109, 111, 114, 117, 121, 125, 126, 142, 143, 146, 148, 150, 153-155, 157, 162, 163, 167, 169-171, 173, 177, 182, 185, 199-202, 207, 212, 220
Pray  29, 37, 77, 95, 112, 116, 122, 141, 159, 183, 187, 222
Prayer  28-30, 38, 43, 48, 62, 75, 76, 96, 107, 119, 127, 130, 154, 162, 163, 167, 181, 186, 207, 222
Priest  38, 60, 70, 90, 114, 152, 153, 164, 171, 181, 187
Priesthood  11, 38, 69, 109
Promise  1, 2, 4, 20, 24, 45, 47, 83, 85-88, 116, 137, 139, 157, 158, 174, 198
Prophet  4, 24, 46, 50, 67, 90, 129, 133, 136, 139, 140, 142, 157, 161, 193, 195
Prophetic  4, 6, 36, 86, 118, 148, 161, 173, 174, 193

R

Reconcile, reconciliation  7, 27 96, 104, 118, 183, 185
Repentance  7, 45, 150, 153, 177, 182
Resurrection  2, 4, 21, 24, 59, 60, 62, 65, 75-77, 79, 83, 87, 88, 90, 91, 93, 97, 100, 106, 110, 114, 158, 168, 176, 182, 195, 197, 198, 203, 207, 212, 214, 215

Sabbath  6, 72
Sacrament(s)  11, 43, 78, 106, 109, 114, 150, 195, 197, 199
Sacrifice  10, 12, 53, 82, 85, 129-132, 161, 198
Salvation  1, 4, 11, 12, 33-35, 37, 42, 43, 45-47, 52, 67, 69, 76, 82, 85, 86, 93, 95, 106, 113, 116-118, 126, 127, 144, 159, 166, 167, 170, 171, 188, 191, 198, 199, 202, 206, 207
Servant  4, 13, 36-38, 40, 42, 43, 45, 59, 61, 65, 102, 105, 183, 216, 217, 219
Service  10, 12, 30, 38, 43, 45, 46, 55, 79, 107, 154, 182, 189, 209, 222
Shepherd  102-105, 221, 222
Sign  36, 47, 59, 75, 77, 96, 104, 105, 113, 160, 171, 174, 180, 181, 206
Silence  24, 62, 76, 83, 130, 148, 160, 161, 163
Sin, sinner  21, 42, 58, 59, 79, 80, 82, 83, 85, 86, 88, 129, 130, 164, 165, 167, 183, 191, 197
Son of God  32, 36, 42, 60, 77, 84, 161, 164, 192
Spirit  16, 24, 26, 35, 42, 47, 52, 57, 76, 77, 87, 95, 106, 108, 117-120, 123, 124, 182, 183, 202, 205, 209, 214, 218
Suffer, suffering  4, 26, 37, 42, 43, 58-63, 65, 80, 82-85, 102, 103, 105, 110, 111, 157, 164, 173, 174, 177, 181, 209

## T

Temptation  58, 59, 79, 107, 173
Theology  48, 52, 80, 170, 178
Transfiguration  62

## V

Values  20, 29, 51, 53, 140, 146, 155, 174, 176, 208, 218
Vatican  10, 38, 169, 178
Vocation  45, 46, 139, 171

## W

Weakness  37, 42, 50, 63, 90, 121, 143, 162-164, 169-171, 189
Wealth  51, 154
Witness  21, 34, 36, 42, 52, 67, 87, 95, 96, 111, 112, 139, 163, 194
Women  10, 47, 59, 66, 67, 69, 83, 84, 91, 127, 143, 180, 188
Word  4, 6, 7, 23-27, 68, 70, 72, 74, 76, 78, 85-87, 97, 98, 100, 101, 106, 109, 110, 112-114, 116-118, 122, 125, 127, 128, 135, 136, 140, 144-146, 148, 153, 157, 159, 162, 164, 170, 195, 207, 209, 213, 221, 222
Word of God  24, 68, 76, 86, 97, 98, 100, 101, 140, 144-146, 148, 153, 209, 213
Work  6, 14, 32, 34, 37, 38, 41, 44, 48, 52, 55, 58, 73, 76, 85, 90, 92, 95, 107, 109, 112, 114, 116, 119, 130, 141, 142, 144, 146, 149, 161, 162, 170, 183, 185-190, 192, 193, 195, 201, 213, 215, 217, 218
World  9, 11-14, 17, 19-22, 24, 27, 28, 30, 32-35, 38, 42, 48, 51, 56-58, 61, 63, 65, 68, 76-80, 83, 84, 86, 91, 95, 106, 110, 111, 113, 114, 116, 118, 119, 121, 123, 126, 127, 130, 131, 138, 139, 142, 143, 145, 146, 152, 155, 159, 166, 170, 171, 174, 177, 185, 194, 197-203, 208, 214, 218, 219, 221
Worship  29, 30, 48, 55, 72, 82, 97, 100, 103, 108, 121, 125, 129, 130, 153, 159, 161, 163, 208

## Y

Yahweh  2, 4, 37, 45, 50, 58, 83, 104, 122, 206